Belgrave Hall, Leicester.

Shire County Guide 29

LEICESTERSHIRE AND RUTLAND

Jeffery Hopewell

Shire Publications Ltd

CONTENTS

1. The changing shires 3
2. The countryside 7
3. Ancient monuments 11
4. Churches 14
5. Historic buildings and gardens 20
6. Museums 26
7. Industrial archaeology 34
8. Other places to visit 39
9. Famous people 41
10. Hunting, cheese and pork pies 45
11. Towns and villages 48
12. Tours for motorists 65
13. Tourist information centres 65
    Map of Leicestershire and Rutland 66
    Index 68

Printed in Great Britain by C. I. Thomas & Sons (Haverfordwest) Ltd, Press Buildings, Merlins Bridge, Haverfordwest, Dyfed SA61 1XF.

British Library Cataloguing in Publication Data: Hopewell, Jeffery. Leicestershire and Rutland. — (Shire County Guide; 29). 1. Leicestershire — Visitors' guide. I. Title. 914.25'404858. ISBN 0-85263-985-6.

Cover: *Normanton Church Water Museum, Rutland Water.*

ACKNOWLEDGEMENTS

Photographs are acknowledged as follows: The Administrator, Belvoir Castle, page 21; The Administrator, Stanford Hall, page 24; Cadbury Lamb, pages 12, 23, 38 (bottom), 39, 58 (bottom), 61 (right); the *Leicester Mercury*, pages 47, 50, 62; copyright Leicestershire Museums, Art Galleries and Records Service, pages 1, 22 (top), 25, 27, 28, 29, 32, 33, 41, 43; John Taylor and Company (Bellfounders) Limited, page 31. All other photographs are by the author. The maps on pages 46, 55 and 66-7 are by D. R. Darton.

Old John, the folly in Bradgate Park, is one of the best known landmarks in Leicestershire.

The Grantham Canal, near Plungar in the Vale of Belvoir, is no longer in use, and sections of it are now without water.

1
The changing shires

Leicestershire and Rutland are not a major tourist area and do not on the whole attract visitors from far away. The locals, however, are well aware of the beauty spots, as the crowded car parks at Foxton Locks and Bradgate Park will testify. There is much that is worthwhile, and one does not have to travel far from any town to find oneself on single-track roads, deep in the countryside.

There is in Leicestershire an east-west divide approximating to the valley of the river Soar and running through the city of Leicester itself. To the west are the granite of Charnwood Forest, the limestone of Breedon on the Hill and the coalfields around Coalville, whereas to the east is the gently rolling countryside stretching into Rutland. These natural features have had a great effect on the type of building and of industry in the county.

The most common building material is probably clay. Because of the shortage of good building stone, this was frequently used for the cottages and boundary walls of poorer people. It was mixed with straw and sometimes dung and gradually built up layer by layer. Some of these buildings still survive, mainly in the south and east of the county. Clay was also used for brick-making in Roman times and then from the late fifteenth century onwards,

Kirby Muxloe Castle being the earliest example, followed by Bradgate House.

Timber was plentiful, especially on the western side, so timber-framed buildings are not unusual in the county. These are usually thatched. Swithland slate was not used for tiles until late in the seventeenth century, and these were too heavy for any but brick and stone buildings. The eastern side had a good supply of ironstone, and there are many houses of this warm-coloured stone. Rutland has limestone quarries in addition, which provided much fine stone, notably at Ketton.

There is evidence of prehistoric settlement in the county and certainly by the bronze age the forests were being cleared and hilltop sites settled, such as Beacon Hill. The hillforts at Breedon and at Burrough are of the iron age, and by the time of the Roman conquest there was a considerable settlement of the Coritani tribe at Leicester. There are three ancient trackways from these pre-Roman times. The Jurassic Trackway enters the county near Husbands Bosworth, going north-east to Kibworth and via Tilton on towards Grantham in Lincolnshire. A second came from the Fens to Croxton Kerrial and across to Six Hills, Barrow and so into Charnwood. Sewstern Lane, or The Drift, begins near Stamford,

Lincolnshire, and follows an almost straight line to Belvoir, before petering out on its way to Newark, Nottinghamshire. It forms the county boundary between Leicestershire and Lincolnshire for much of its length, which is a sure sign of its antiquity.

The Romans adopted parts of these older roads but built many more themselves. The Fosse Way, from Exeter to Lincoln, runs from High Cross in the south to Six Hills in the north and is the longest stretch of Roman road in the county. It starts as a bridle track and picks up the B4114 north of Sharnford. The exact line is lost at Enderby but it clearly emerges from Leicester as the A46. The Watling Street (A5), from London to Wroxeter, Shropshire, forms the south-western border of the county, and the Ermine Street (A1), from London to York, passes through the eastern part of Rutland. The Gartree Road, now mainly a minor road or bridleway, runs south-east from Leicester by Great Stretton and on to Medbourne, ultimately reaching Colchester, Essex. Another road leads from Leicester to Mancetter, Warwickshire, where Boudicca's revolt was finally crushed.

This road network points to the importance of Roman Leicester (*Ratae Coritanorum*), where substantial remains can be seen, notably the Jewry Wall and the mosaics in the adjacent museum. Three settlements lie on the Watling Street: *Tripontium*, near Shawell, *Venonis* (High Cross) and *Manduessedum* (Mancetter, although much of the site is at Witherley). There are both a military camp and a villa at Great Casterton and further excavations have been carried out at other sites, including Thistleton, Medbourne and Goadby Marwood.

The transition from the declining Roman rule to Saxon domination seems to have been gradual, with evidence of continuing Saxon occupation of Roman sites. Villages with place-names ending in -ham may date from this period, such as Keyham, North Luffenham and Wymondham. Many Saxon cemeteries have been excavated, notably at Thurmaston and Empingham, where some fine gilt-bronze cruciform brooches were found. Leicestershire became part of the kingdom of Mercia and there may have been royal palaces at Gumley and Great Glen. Saint Wistan, a Mercian prince, was murdered at Wistow in AD 849.

The Danes conquered the East Midlands in 877. There are few archaeological traces of their tenure beyond a scattering of settlements, recognisable by the endings -by or -thorpe, such as Ingarsby and Osgathorpe. Danish rule lasted only until 918, when the Mercian kingdom regained the area. The best places to see Saxon architecture are the churches of Breedon on the Hill and St

Nicholas, Leicester.

The Norman conquest brought over a new aristocracy, including Robert de Todeni, who built the first Belvoir castle. Other motte and bailey castles were erected, such as Leicester, Castle Donington, Hallaton and Sauvey. Land was granted to monastic foundations, and there were at one time over forty religious houses in Leicestershire and Rutland. It has been calculated that their annual income was about one fifth of the total for the whole of the two counties. Markets flourished not only in the towns but in villages as small as Lowesby and Scalford. Life was not easy, however, especially for those living within reach of Ashby Folville, home of the Folville family who terrorised the neighbourhood in the early fourteenth century.

Around this time there was a decline in the population and after the Black Death of 1348-9 and two further plagues the population was only half or two-thirds of what it had been at the beginning of the fourteenth century. Curiously, only one village, Ambion, half-way between Shenton and Dadlington, seems to have disappeared at this time. Most of the 65 settlements now deserted became depopulated between 1450 and 1550, largely as a result of enclosure, as at Ingarsby and Whatborough.

The Wars of the Roses affected most of England at some time or another. In Rutland there was a battle near Pickworth in 1470, known as the battle of Loosecoat Field because the defeated Lancastrians hurried to tear off the coats which identified them as being on the losing side. The battle of Bosworth in 1485 is the most famous battle fought on Leicestershire soil; it led to the coronation of Henry VII and ended the Wars of the Roses.

His son, Henry VIII, instigated the Reformation and the Dissolution of the Monasteries, giving local landowners the chance to buy up monastic lands cheaply. Leicestershire had long been a hotbed of religious dissent, going back as far as Wyclif, and gave the Church of England one of its most notable martyrs, Hugh Latimer. The Tudor dynasty was not secure, and an unfortunate victim of the politics of the time was Lady Jane Grey. Mary, Queen of Scots, was kept for some time at Ashby de la Zouch.

Ashby played a large part in the Civil War and the Royalist garrison was besieged several times, as was that at Belvoir. Both castles were rendered defenceless after they were captured. Leicester itself was strongly Parliamentarian, and was taken by the King in 1645. His triumph was short-lived, for after the débâcle of Naseby just over the Northamptonshire border he and Prince Rupert were forced to flee, pausing at Wistow, where Sir Richard Halford gave them fresh horses, before pressing on to Ashby. Leicester was recaptured four

*Left: A pagan goddess of uncertain date, by the church tower at Braunston, Rutland.
Right: A Saxon sculpture of the Virgin Mary at Breedon on the Hill.*

days later.

It took some time for the city to recover its prosperity, but, by the time Daniel Defoe visited it, early in the eighteenth century, he could write: 'They have considerable manufacture carried on here, and in several of the market towns round, for weaving of stockings by frames; and one would scarce think it possible so small an article of trade could employ such multitudes of people as it does; for the whole county seems to be employed in it.' He also commented on the fine sheep, cattle and horses of the county and noted dismissively that 'Mount Sorrel, Loughborough, Melton Mowbray, and Waltham in the Would . . . are market towns, but of no great note.'

Later in the century, as the industrial revolution gathered momentum, a canal network was built to complement the navigable rivers in moving goods around the country and improving trade. The Grand Union Canal still survives, but the Grantham, Charnwood Forest and Oakham Canals are derelict. The Oakham Canal was the first to be taken over by a railway company and the Midland Railway laid its track on part of its course in 1846. The canals could not compete with the railways, which provided a much faster service to more places. Even so, some railways were unable to make a profit, and over the years many miles of track have been closed.

Leicester grew at a rapid rate. The population was about 6000 at the beginning of the eighteenth century, 17,000 in 1801, 60,000 by about 1850, and, having swallowed up several older villages, 219,000 by 1901. Hosiery remained the major industry but the manufacture of footwear increased considerably in the latter half of the century. Engineering and ironfounding were also to the fore, with foundries not only at Leicester, but also at Moira, Loughborough (notably Taylor's bell foundry), Lutterworth and Asfordby. The iron ore for these foundries was quarried both in the west of Leicestershire and in Rutland, with the last workings closing in 1974. Limestone is still quarried in both areas, and there are plenty of granite quarries in full production in the west of the county. The coal mines in the Coalville area are approaching exhaustion, but new mines are to be opened in the Vale of Belvoir, near Asfordby.

Changes occurred in the rural areas as well. The enclosure of the old open fields started in the late middle ages, and by the end of the seventeenth century over half of the county had been enclosed. By the end of the following century almost all the open fields had been divided and were criss-crossed by hedges and ditches. Curiously, Medbourne managed to remain unchanged until 1844. Enclosure creates good hunting country with stout hedges for jumping. Since enclosure had done away with a number of small spinneys, the hunts planted fox covers to replace them, to be sure of somewhere to find a fox. Botany Bay on the road from Houghton on the Hill to Tilton is one such, made in about 1790, when the convict colony was founded. Another is Grimston Gorse, above the tunnel on the old Midland Railway line from Melton Mowbray to Nottingham. This was formerly known as Brudenell's Gorse, as it was planted by James Brudenell, Earl of Cardigan.

The pattern of farming has changed too. At the beginning of the twentieth century eighty per cent of agricultural land was grazing, but helped by the drive for food production of two world wars, this has decreased to about fifty per cent. Windmills and watermills have been superseded, though Claybrooke Mill is once more grinding flour. Local breweries, formerly declining, are now fighting back with the demand for 'real ale', and the beer from Ruddle's in Rutland is known throughout Britain. Indeed, their 'Rutland Bitter' and the much contested 'Rutland Water' were a great help in keeping the county in the public eye when it seemed as if it would disappear altogether in the boundary changes of 1974 that relegated it to become a district of Leicestershire.

Change is a feature of this age, but there are parts of the city, the towns, the villages and the countryside of Leicestershire and Rutland where change has happened at a slower pace. It is still possible to discover quiet corners and beautiful scenery to match anywhere else in England.

Left: *The half-timbered gatehouse to Leicester Castle.*
Right: *The statue of Richard III, by James Butler RA, in the Castle Gardens, Leicester.*

The outcrops of Beacon Hill.

2
The countryside

Beacon Hill, Woodhouse Eaves (OS 129: SK 511147). Leicestershire County Council. 1 mile west of Woodhouse Eaves on B591. Main car park is just north of the road.

Beacon Hill is a beauty spot with panoramic views of Charnwood Forest but is also interesting from the point of view of its archaeology, geology and natural history. The area was settled in the early bronze age, and a flat axe head of the period has been found on this site. A small hoard of late bronze age implements has also been discovered and the low, rather overgrown ramparts surrounding the hilltop may well be of the same period. The crags of Beacon Hill are of volcanic ash about 700 million years old and are noted for the fossils that have been found there. The hill is mainly covered with bracken and various grasses but heather can still be seen in places. Some parts are rather boggy and there are several ponds. The lower slopes are wooded and have a variety of trees and shrubs, some of which, such as rhododendrons, were planted in the nineteenth century, when it was part of the Beaumanor Estate.

Bradgate Park, Newtown Linford (OS 140: SK 523097). The main car park is by the church in Newtown Linford, but there are two more: at Hunts Hill about a mile from Newtown Linford on the road towards Swithland, and at Hallgates about a mile west of Cropston by the reservoir on B5330. Information centre at Marion's Cottage, by the Newtown Linford car park.

This is the largest park in Leicestershire covering some 800 acres (320 ha), and, because of its proximity to Leicester, the most popular. It is part of the same range of volcanic rock as Beacon Hill and has a similar mixture of heath, bracken and grass-covered slopes, with rocky outcrops and clumps of woodland. There is a deer sanctuary and red and fallow deer can often be seen at close quarters, quite unperturbed by the influx of visitors. The park overlooks Cropston Reservoir, where there is a variety of waterfowl. It was enclosed before 1247 and gives a good impression of what a medieval hunting park was like. It belonged to the Grey family, one of whom, Thomas, first Marquess of Dorset, built one of the first unfortified brick country houses here in 1490. This remained the family seat until 1719 and thereafter was left to degenerate into the ruin that can now be seen. Three towers of the west wing still stand quite high and inside is the massive kitchen fireplace. The south-east tower of the east wing remains, as does the chapel with its monument to Henry Grey, who died in 1614, and his wife. Bradgate was the home of Lady Jane Grey (see chapter 9). The other curious building in the park is a stone folly at the top of a hill. It is known as Old John and was built on the site of a disused windmill in 1784 by the fifth Earl of Stamford in memory of an old retainer.

Deer grazing in Bradgate Park.

Broombriggs Farm and Windmill Hill, Woodhouse Eaves (OS 129: SK 523144). Leicestershire County Council. Car park ½ mile west of Woodhouse Eaves on the south side of the B591.

Broombriggs is a mixed arable and stock farm with a farm trail about 1½ miles long, with plaques to point out the major items of interest along the way. There are also picnic areas and a network of other tracks for riders and walkers. On Windmill Hill stands the stone roundhouse of a wooden post mill destroyed by fire in 1945. There are fine views of Charnwood from this spot.

Groby Pool, Groby (OS 140: SK 520080). The car park is just off the road from Groby to Newtown Linford.

Groby (pronounced 'Grooby') Pool is the largest natural lake in the county. It is privately owned but can be seen from the adjacent footpath. It is a good place for all kinds of waterfowl and sometimes kingfishers have been seen.

The Jubilee Way

The Jubilee Way was opened in 1977 to mark the Queen's Silver Jubilee and is 15½ miles (25 km) long, mainly using public footpaths. It starts in Melton Mowbray, heading north to Scalford, Goadby Marwood and Eaton. It then meanders till it reaches wood-land north-west of Eaton and continues through the woods until it passes Belvoir Castle (see chapter 5). From there it crosses into Lincolnshire at Woolsthorpe, joining the Viking Way at Brewer's Grave. The county council has produced an excellent pamphlet giving detailed directions and highlighting points of interest along the way.

The Leicestershire Round

The Leicestershire Footpath Association has devised a circular walk, taking in many of the county's more interesting sights. For those who find the prospect of 100 miles (160 km) too daunting, the walk has been split into small sections, most between 2½ and 4 miles (4-6 km) long. The first part starts at Burrough Hill (see chapter 3) and makes its way to Foxton Locks (see chapter 7) via Owston (see chapter 3), Launde, Hallaton and the Langtons (all described in chapter 11). The next part goes on to High Cross, the junction of two Roman roads — the Watling Street and the Fosse Way — and across Bosworth Field (see chapter 8) to the town of Market Bosworth (see chapter 11). The final part takes the walker past the Battlefield Line at Shackerstone (see chapter 8), Thornton (see chapter 4), Newtown Linford (see chapter 11), Bradgate Park, Broombriggs and Beacon Hill (all described above), Mountsorrel (see chapter 11), along the Wreake valley and on to Gaddesby (see chapter 4), finishing at Burrough Hill. Each part is described in detail, with accompanying maps, in three booklets published by Leicestershire Libraries and Information Service.

Market Bosworth Country Park, Market Bosworth (OS 140: SK 413032). Leicestershire County Council. Car park on B585 just east of Market Bosworth.

This was once part of a large deer park established in 1665 and later landscaped in the late eighteenth-century style. Its 87 acres (35 ha) are mainly mature parkland with a lake and several streams and ponds. What was once an area of mixed woodland is now being replanted as an arboretum with oaks and maples.

The Outwoods, Woodhouse Lane, Loughborough (OS 129: SK 515159). Charnwood Borough Council. Car park on the minor road between Nanpantan and Woodhouse Eaves.

These woods, about 100 acres (40 ha) of oaks and conifers, are on a long ridge of high ground overlooking Loughborough and the Soar valley. There are many walks and rides within the woods and also footpaths and a bridleway into Loughborough.

Rutland Water, Whitwell, Oakham, Rutland LE15 8BW. Anglian Water Authority — Oundle Division. Telephone: 078086 321. There are four car parks, each with a picnic area: Normanton car park, near Edith Weston, and three just off A606 Oakham to Stamford road, at Barnsdale, Whitwell and

Sykes Lane, which is halfway between Whitwell and Empingham. The information centre is at Sykes Lane.

Rutland Water is the largest man-made lake in Europe, covering 3100 acres (1260 ha) and storing 27,300 million gallons (124 million cubic metres) of water. It was built in the early 1970s to provide water for Leicestershire, Northamptonshire, parts of Lincolnshire, Milton Keynes and Peterborough. As well as its primary function as a reservoir it is also a major water sports and leisure centre. There is sailing, canoeing and windsurfing and, for those who feel less active, a pleasure cruiser does regular round trips. Rutland Water has been well stocked with trout and day fishing permits are obtainable. Bicycles can be hired for a leisurely cycle ride on the 15 miles (24 km) of track around the waterside. Gardeners will be interested in the Drought Garden, which has been laid out to display plants that require little watering and special techniques for conserving water. An arboretum contains the 22 different species of tree that have been used in the landscaping of Rutland Water.

A mile-long nature trail has been laid out between the Barnsdale and Whitwell car parks, but more importantly the western ends of the reservoir have been retained as nature reserves and no other activities are permitted nearby. Visitors are allowed into both the Egleton and Lyndon Hill reserves and the Visitor Centre at the latter demonstrates the variety of wildlife and the importance of conservation. Over 220 species of birds have been recorded at Rutland Water including

Windsurfers and yachts on Rutland Water.

great northern divers and ospreys. It is surprising how many seabirds turn up here. A number of waterfowl, notably gadwall, mute swan, shoveller and tufted duck, breed here and waders and gulls are well represented. All sorts of other birds nest around the shores and it is a convenient port of call for migrants.

The half-submerged church at Normanton is an unusual landmark. This houses the water museum described in chapter 6.

Swithland Woods, Swithland (OS 129: SK 538118). Bradgate Park Trustees. Car parks on B5330 about 1¼ miles north-west of Cropston and about 1 mile west of Swithland on the road to Newtown Linford.

This is a remnant of the ancient Charnwood Forest, covering 146 acres (59 ha), and is mainly of oak with some alder, ash, birch and lime. Within the woods are two deep water-filled quarries, from which came the famous Swithland slate used for roofing and for gravestones. There is a variety of soils and hence a variety of plant life including uncommon species such as betony, saw-wort and adder's tongue. The woods are also noted for their birds, butterflies and moths.

The Viking Way

This is a long-distance footpath from the Humber Bridge to Oakham, 120 miles (193 km) in all. The Leicestershire section is 24 miles (38 km) long. From Oakham it skirts the northern edge of Rutland Water and then heads north to Exton, with its notable church (see chapter 4). From there it goes to Thistleton via Greetham. Thistleton is famous as the venue for the prize fight in 1811 between Tom Cribb and Tom Molyneux. Here the Viking Way picks up the prehistoric road that runs from Stamford to Newark, known as The Drift or Sewstern Lane, Sewstern being the only village on the road for many miles. A sign of its antiquity is that it forms the boundary between Leicestershire and Lincolnshire. Just north of Saltby airfield are King Lud's Entrenchments, a bank with two ditches, that would seem to be a boundary of the middle bronze age. The road continues north-north-west to Woolsthorpe, joining the Jubilee Way east of the village at Brewer's Grave. The Viking Way is waymarked and Leicestershire County Council has issued a leaflet giving details of the route.

Windswept hawthorns on the ramparts of Burrough Hill.

10

Sheep graze over the deserted village of Ingarsby, with Ingarsby Old Hall in the background.

3
Ancient monuments

Breedon Hill, Breedon on the Hill (OS 129: SK 406234).

This site has been occupied since the stone age, but it is best known as an iron age hillfort. The ramparts can clearly be seen in a crescent shape west of the church; the eastern side has been quarried away throughout the twentieth century. There have been several excavations carried out which have produced much iron age pottery and a large number of querns.

Burrough Hill, Burrough on the Hill (OS 129: SK 761118). Leicestershire County Council. A car park is provided on the road between Somerby and Burrough on the Hill.

Set on a natural promontory, this iron age hillfort commands magnificent views of all the surrounding countryside and on a clear day one can see Leicester and Charnwood Forest to the west, Billesdon Coplow (see chapter 11) and beyond to the south, far into Rutland on the east and Melton Mowbray to the north. The fort is particularly impressive with its high earthworks and must have been practically impregnable when its ramparts were topped by a timber palisade. Excavations around the east gateway have revealed a cobbled road and the foundations of a gatehouse, and elsewhere traces of continuous occupation from the early bronze age to the fourth century AD have been found. In Tudor times and probably earlier people would gather from far and wide at Whitsuntide for dancing and sporting competitions. Later the Melton Hunt Races were held around the site.

Grace Dieu Priory, near Thringstone (OS 129: SK 435183).

The priory was founded about 1235-40 by Roesia de Verdun for nuns of the Augustinian order and was sold at the Reformation to John Beaumont of Thringstone for his personal use. It later passed into the hands of Sir Ambrose Phillipps, who pulled most of it down, though the ruins can still be seen standing from the A512. They represent part of the chapter house, cloister and dormitory.

Great Stretton (OS 141: SK 656004).

All the hallmarks of a classic deserted village can be seen at Great Stretton: an isolated church, village earthworks, a moated site and fishpond all bounded by fields of ridge and furrow. There are house sites and streets to the north-east and south of the church and about 200 yards (180 metres) south is the moated manor site and fishpond.

Hallaton Castle, Hallaton (OS 141: SP 780967).

The mound that remains was first excavated in 1878 when it was thought to be a 'British

The Jewry Wall, Leicester, and, behind it, St Nicholas church.

camp'. It is in fact a twelfth-century motte and bailey castle, probably built during the troubled reign of King Stephen (1135-54) to protect the surrounding iron workings. It appears to have fallen into disuse by the end of the twelfth century though the iron workings may well have continued for some time.

Hamilton, near Scraptoft (OS 140: SK 643073).

This village was deserted in the mid fifteenth century, but a clear grid of its streets may still be seen together with the outlines of about ten houses, the manor house and the chapel. The surrounding fields retain their medieval ridge and furrow contours.

Ingarsby, near Houghton on the Hill (OS 141: SK 685052).

Ingarsby is best viewed coming from Houghton on the Hill, walking uphill from the stream towards Ingarsby Old Hall. On the left is a large sunken area with hawthorns growing around the perimeter. This was the mill pond. On the right the plan of the village, streets, lanes and house sites can be made out. The village was depopulated in 1469 when the Abbey of Leicester, which owned the manor, enclosed the land for sheep and cattle farming. The east wing of the Old Hall may have been built in the late fifteenth century by the abbey for its bailiff, or by Brian Cave, who bought the manor after the Dissolution of the Monas-

teries in the 1540s. Opposite are further earthworks which were probably stock enclosures.

Leicester Jewry Wall, St Nicholas Circle (OS 140: SK 582043).

The name of this remnant of Roman Leicester has nothing to do with the Jews but is probably associated with the aldermen (Jurats) of the medieval town. When the site was first excavated in 1936 it was thought to be the forum, but this lay a little to the east, now cut through by Southgates Underpass. It is, however, the next most important building for any Roman town — the baths. The site has been left exposed and is well signed. The Jewry Wall itself is the wall between the baths and the *palaestra* (exercise hall), now covered by St Nicholas church.

Leicester: Raw Dykes, Aylestone Road (OS 140: SK 584026).

These earthworks once extended much further into Leicester but now only a short stretch remains. Their exact purpose is unknown but it has been suggested that they are the remains of a Roman aqueduct bringing water into the town from the Knighton Brook. Prince Rupert used part of the Raw Dykes nearer the city as a redoubt for his cannon when he laid siege to it in 1645.

Leicester: The Abbey, Abbey Park Road (OS 140: SK 585060).

Robert le Bossu founded the abbey in 1143

for the Augustinians and it rapidly became one of the richest and most powerful in the county. It is the burial place of the disgraced Cardinal Wolsey, who died in 1530 as he was making his way back to London to answer a charge of high treason. The abbey did not survive long as it was dissolved in 1538 and the site passed through several hands before being bought in 1551 by the Earl of Huntingdon, who built Cavendish House from the remains. This house was burnt down in the Civil War, though not completely destroyed, and its ruins are still quite impressive. Not so the abbey, whose plan, marked out on the lawns, is disputed.

Owston Abbey, Owston (OS 141: SK 774079).
The Augustinian abbey was founded here by Robert Grimbald shortly before 1161. It was in decline even before the Dissolution of the Monasteries and all that remains above ground is the nave, north aisle and north-west tower, which have been made into the parish church. The bulk of this is thirteenth century, partly obscured by successive restorations. The rest of the buildings have disappeared though a fine series of fishponds lies to the south of the church.

Sauvey Castle (OS 141: SK 786053).
The earliest reference to Sauvey is in 1211 when King John's accounts record the expenditure of £442 13s 1d incurred in building it. The castle changed hands several times during the next fifty years but quickly outlived its usefulness and was left to decay. The castle is of the motte and bailey type, built between the fork of two streams which provide a natural moat. A large cross ditch on the west side completes the defences. An inner court stands slightly

higher than the rest and the site of the chapel, built in 1244, can be seen in the middle.

Theddingworth (OS 141: SP 666858).
The medieval settlement, with its main north-south street and smaller lanes at right angles, is best seen from the disused level-crossing on the Theddingworth to Laughton road towards the present village, which lies along the main road.

Ulverscroft Priory (OS 129: SK 501127). The priory stands on private property but may be seen from the public footpath alongside.
This is the most substantial monastic ruin in the county but even so is by no means complete. The priory was founded by Robert le Bossu in 1134 and was taken over by the Augustinian order forty years later. This was by far the most notable order in Leicestershire with a total of eleven houses of which Ulverscroft was one of the smallest. The site is bounded by a moat and fishponds and the most impressive remains are of the church, with its west tower and south wall still standing. Close to the tower is the guest house, which is basically thirteenth-century, and at right angles is the refectory of a similar date.

Wing, Rutland (OS 141: SK 895028).
A curious circular maze about 40 feet (12 metres) in diameter, cut into the turf, dates back to the middle ages. Its exact purpose is unknown, but because similar maze patterns are found on the floors of several French cathedrals it has been suggested that wrong-doers submitted to penance by crawling on hands and knees around the maze. Similar mazes once existed at Medbourne and Lyddington.

The turf maze at Wing.

4
Churches

Bottesford: St Mary.

The spire of this church is the highest in the county at 207 feet (63 metres) and can be seen for miles around. The rest of the building is largely fourteenth-century, with both north and south aisles and transepts. The grand exterior has interesting gargoyles and a decorative frieze. The interior is comparatively plain and the only furnishings of note are the late sixteenth-century font and the pulpit and reading desk of 1631. The monuments in the chancel, however, are worthy of a visit in their own right. The earliest is a miniature effigy of Robert de Roos (died 1285), the next of an unknown lady of about 1310-20. There are brasses to two rectors, Henry de Codyngton (died 1404), magnificent in his cope and standing under an ornate canopy, and a much smaller figure to John Freeman (died 1420). Two alabaster knights on tomb-chests represent William and John Lord Roos (died 1414 and 1421), but all these are almost eclipsed by the monuments to the first eight Earls of Rutland. These dominate the chancel, reflecting the importance of the family. The first Earl

The alewife: a gargoyle on Bottesford church.

(died 1543) lies with his wife on a tomb-chest with mourners, whereas the second Earl (died 1563) lies with his wife under a table-tomb with their children kneeling on top. The third and fourth Earls died within a year of each other, 1587 and 1588, and are commemorated with their wives by monuments carved by Gerard Johnson. A similar tomb by Nicholas Johnson was erected for the fifth Earl (died 1612) and his wife. By far the most grandiose monument is the tomb to the sixth Earl (died 1632), which reaches to the roof of the chancel. His two wives are also shown, and the inscription refers to two of his children being killed by witchcraft. The last two monuments were carved by Grinling Gibbons in the 1680s and depict the seventh Earl (died 1641) and the eighth Earl (died 1679) and his wife, all in Roman garments.

Breedon on the Hill: St Mary and St Hardulph.

Standing on an iron age hillfort, overlooking the surrounding countryside, this church is an impressive sight. It was founded late in the seventh century by monks from Peterborough. Nothing survives from this early date but there is some fine Saxon sculpture of the ninth century. About 63 feet (19 metres) of wall frieze remains, with interlacing and decorative designs, together with birds, beasts, a knight charging on horseback and a kneeling spearman. Fragments of three crosses show more interlacing and beasts, a panel of Adam and Eve being tempted by the serpent and a curious panel of a pagan warrior being offered a drinking horn. The finest sculptures are a half-figure of the Virgin Mary flanked by saints, and the Archangel Gabriel raising his right hand in blessing. A Norman doorway may be seen on the north side of the tower, but the rest of the church is thirteenth-century and is the former chancel of the priory. Nothing remains of the original nave. The fifteenth-century octagonal font has some fine decoration and heraldic shields. The box pews, pulpit, reading desk and west gallery are all of the eighteenth century, but more magnificent is the Shirley family pew of 1627 with its elaborate canopy and coats of arms. The three Elizabethan alabaster monuments are all to members of this family. Note especially the tomb of George Shirley (died 1622) and his wife (died 1595) that was erected in 1598. They and their two sons and daughter kneel on the upper tier whilst a skeleton lies below on a slab.

Brooke: St Peter.

The earliest part of this church is the

The church at Breedon on the Hill.

Norman doorway, the tower being thirteenth-century and the nave about a century later. The north aisle and chapel and the chancel were all rebuilt in 1579 and most of the interior woodwork is of the same date, although the pulpit and altar rails are of the early 1600s. It is a delight to enter this church, for it seems nothing has altered for four centuries. The square font is Norman and also worthy of note is the monument to Charles Noel (died 1619).

Claybrooke Parva: St Peter.

Most of the church dates from the late thirteenth century but its main attraction is its large chancel of about 1340 with three tall windows on each side, all with identical flowing tracery and a few fragments of the original stained glass. The majority of the fittings belong to the restoration of 1876-8.

Eastwell: St Michael.

This church is unusual in that the chancel was built first, probably in about 1220, and the nave added later in the same century. Rather than demolish the wall between them, it was decided to cut an archway and two windows, and it became the screen. The south aisle is of about the same date whereas the north aisle is fifteenth-century and the clerestory a little later still. In the north wall of the chancel is a fourteenth-century figure of a priest holding a chalice. The rather fine cast iron lectern was given in 1861.

Exton: St Peter and St Paul.

The church now appears Victorian, since much had to be rebuilt after the spire was struck by lightning in 1843 and fell on the nave. Little of the fourteenth-century building remains, but note the carvings on the columns of the north aisle. However, the main attraction is not the architecture of the church, nor its charming setting in parkland, but its fine series of sixteenth- to eighteenth-century monuments to members of the Harington and Noel families. John Harington (died 1524) lies in full armour and his wife, Alice, has two small lap dogs at her feet. Their grandson James (died 1591) kneels opposite his wife, Lucy, in a large Elizabethan wall monument, and their grandson Kelway, who died in infancy, lies with his maternal grandfather, Robert Kelway (died 1580), in an even more impressive monument that fills the wall of the south transept. Another relative, Lady Anne Bruce (died 1627), lies peacefully in her shroud on a tomb-chest. James Noel (died 1681) stands contemplating two cherubic brothers who died young, but his monument is completely overshadowed by the huge one by Grinling Gibbons to the third Viscount Campden (died 1683), his four wives and nineteen children. The remaining two monuments are by Nollekens with allegorical figures and portrait medallions of the deceased, Lieutenant-General Bennett Noel (died 1766) and the Countess of Gainsborough (died 1771) and her two husbands.

15

The monument to Colonel Cheney in Gaddesby church.

Gaddesby: St Luke.

The Knights Templar owned several estates in Leicestershire and were lords of the manor of Gaddesby, so it may be due to them that the mainly thirteenth-century church was further enlarged and lavishly decorated in the following century. The south aisle has a curved triangular window at the west end and rich canopy work which continues eastwards but stops abruptly before reaching the end of the aisle. It may be that work was interrupted by the Black Death. The earliest form of seating in the church is the stone ledge around the walls and at the base of pillars, but there are also eighteen benches of such crude workmanship that they must be medieval. The church has a good font and several monuments, including one to Colonel Cheney, who fought at the Battle of Waterloo. That day four of the horses he rode were killed and the almost life-size statue depicts one of them sinking to the ground with his rider, drawing his sword, still in the saddle.

King's Norton: St John Baptist.

This is one of the finest eighteenth-century churches in England and is seen at its best when approached from the south. It was built in a strict Gothic-Revival style by the Leicestershire architect John Wing the younger for the local squire William Fortrey between 1757 and 1775. It was once even more impressive, originally having a tall slender spire, which fell in a severe storm in 1850, destroying the organ in the west gallery and the font which stood beneath it. The rest of the fittings remain unaltered — box pews and a central three-decker pulpit flanked by small gates leading to the chancel area, where the pews are arranged college-wise, at right angles to the communion rails and panelled sanctuary. The poverty of the tiny parish ensured the escape of the church from restoration so fortunately no stained glass mars its light spacious interior. Even the Victorian font in the Christening pew under the west gallery does not look out of place.

Leicester. See chapter 11.

Lockington: St Nicholas.

The present church was first built in the thirteenth century, enlarged in the fourteenth and the tower and clerestory were added in the fifteenth. Little of the fabric has been altered since then. It still has the original Norman font as well as a Georgian replacement in alabaster and some interesting woodwork. The chancel screen and the parclose screen are both fifteenth-century and there are some benches of about 1500. The west gallery and the two-decker pulpit are both eighteenth-century. The communion rail dates from the time of Archbishop Laud and there are a few slightly earlier box pews. The church was once full of box pews and a nineteenth-century rector, the

16

Reverend John Story, used one as a cockpit when he pitted one of his prize fighting-cocks against one belonging to the Marquis of Hastings. Most box pews disappeared in an unfortunate restoration of the church in the 1950s as did six of the eleven incised slabs. Of those that remain two are worth seeing — Robert Stals, a priest in mass vestments holding a chalice, who died in 1540, and Thomas Malle and his wife, of 1545. There are also monuments to Elizabeth Langham (died 1501), who lies on a tomb-chest with mourners, and William Bainbrigge (died 1614), kneeling with his thirteen children. The most striking feature inside the church is, however, the enormous composition above the chancel screen. The royal arms of Queen Anne, dated 1704, perch above boards displaying the Ten Commandments, the Creed and the Lord's Prayer.

Lubenham: All Saints.

This is a rather homely church, typical of many village churches with its squat tower, warm stonework and two monstrous gargoyles on the north of the clerestory. Its oldest features are the two very solid pillars between the nave and the north aisle, which date from the twelfth or thirteenth century. What gives it atmosphere is the interior of 1810 — box pews and a tall pulpit with sounding board, white walls and mainly clear glass. In addition it has a few medieval bench ends, a decorated sixteenth-century chest and a Jacobean family pew in what remains of the south aisle.

Lyddington: St Andrew.

In the middle ages the Bishops of Lincoln stayed in the Bede House (see chapter 5), which is why this church appears grander than expected in a small village. It is basically a fourteenth-century building remodelled in the late fifteenth century, with slender pillars and a clerestory. Of this date, too, are the lower part of the screen, with its partly defaced paintings of saints, and the wall paintings; but the two most unusual features of the church are in the chancel itself. High up in the walls may be seen holes for acoustic jars, an early device for amplifying the voice of the priest, but more noticeable is the unique arrangement of the 1635 communion rails which surround the altar. This was the compromise worked out by Bishop Williams of Lincoln, whose puritan views dictated that the Lord's Table should be free-standing in the centre of the chancel, when faced with an order from William Laud, the Archbishop of Canterbury, that the altar should be against the east wall and separated from the rest of the chancel by a rail.

Mount St Bernard (Roman Catholic).

The abbey was founded in 1835 for Cistercian monks and was the first to be built since the Reformation. The architect, Pugin, had grandiose plans but these could not be fully carried out through lack of funds. Only the nave and aisles of the church were built then. In the 1930s the nave was turned into the monastic choir and work was continued eastwards, adding a solid tower, with the sanctuary area beneath and a nave for the laity. Just north of the church is a rocky outcrop with a calvary.

Staunton Harold: Holy Trinity.

It is most surprising to discover that this church was built in 1653; indeed, it is the only church in England built during the Commonwealth that survives complete with its original fittings. Sir Robert Shirley, an ardent Royalist, founded it as a statement of faith and, having incurred the displeasure of Cromwell, died in the Tower three years later. The style of the building is entirely Gothic — west tower, nave with clerestory and aisles, and chancel. Inside, the fittings are distinctly seventeenth-century. The organ sits in the handsome west gallery with a screen beneath and the walls are panelled throughout. Note the painted ceilings. The box pews all face towards the pulpit and reading desk but the eye is drawn towards

King's Norton church, built in 1760.

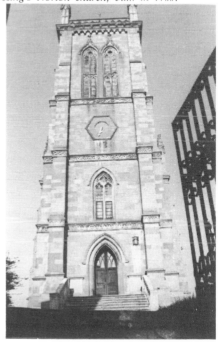

17

Staunton Harold church, seen from across the lake.

the early eighteenth-century wrought iron screen, which was probably commissioned by another Robert Shirley (died 1714), whose monument is in the chancel.

Stoke Dry: St Andrew.

Of the Norman church little remains but it is of outstanding interest. Either side of the chancel arch are barbaric carvings of about 1120 with angels, devils, a dragon, a lion, an eagle, a man peering through foliage and a bellringer. The rest of the church is mainly thirteenth-century, with a fifteenth-century clerestory and porch with an upper room. Inside there is much to see: the woodwork — screen, bench ends and seventeenth-century communion rail — and especially the wall paintings and monuments. The paintings are in the chancel and side chapel and are probably of the same date as the main church building. One can make out quite clearly the Virgin and Child, the crucifixion of St Andrew, St Edmund, St Christopher and St Margaret. The monuments are all to the Digby family: an incised slab to Jaquet (died 1496); Everard (died 1540), whose effigy lies on a tomb-chest; and Kenelm (died 1590) and his wife, Anne (died 1602), who also lie on a tomb-chest with their children standing upright around the sides, including an infant in swaddling clothes.

Stoke Golding: St Margaret.

This church was built in the thirteenth century; first the nave and chancel, then a little later the south aisle and chapel, which are as high and wide as the nave itself. The chancel was rebuilt in 1882 but fortunately the fine east window survives. All the windows have good tracery, especially on the south side. Those on the north do not have the same rhythm and are early fourteenth-century, put in at the same time as the tower was built. The pillars inside the church are very finely carved, mainly with foliage and a variety of human heads. Apart from the fourteenth-century font with its figures of St Margaret, St Catharine and a bishop, the fittings are rather disappointing.

Teigh: Holy Trinity.

Only the lower stages of the tower are left from the medieval church; the rest was built in 1782 with nave and chancel under one roof. Inside, the pews are arranged facing inwards as in a college chapel and the pulpit is high on the west wall flanked by two reading desks. The 'window' behind them with a view of trees beyond is in fact painted! Either side are the Lord's Prayer and the Creed. Similarly the Ten Commandments are inscribed on either side of the real east window. There are two fonts — a mahogany one of vase shape which would be fixed to the altar rails when required, and a stone one carved by the rector of the church in 1845.

Thornton: St Peter.

Like so many churches in the county this church was built about 1300 with further work carried out around 1500 when the tower and spire were rebuilt and the clerestory added. At about the same time the font and screen were made; the latter retains much of its original colouring. The bench ends with linenfold panelling are later — about 1560. The heavy south door is fourteenth-century and said to have come from Ulverscroft Priory. There are some roundels of stained glass of a similar date in the south aisle, depicting two Magi, the Virgin and the Flight into Egypt.

Tickencote: St Peter.

The nave of the Norman chapel was rebuilt in the late middle ages and the whole church was restored and rebuilt in 1792. The architect seems to have kept reasonably close to the original design of the chancel but made the nave conform to his ideal of the Norman style, which has a certain appeal even if it is somewhat inaccurate. Inside, the Norman chancel arch is stunning for such a tiny church, having six concentric orders of decoration, one with a variety of grotesques. The chancel itself is remarkable for its Norman vaulting with a central boss carved with three curious heads.

Tilton on the Hill: St Peter.

Tilton is the highest village in the county, at about 700 feet (215 metres) above sea level, and its church is the high point of the village. It is built in honey-coloured ironstone and dates back to the end of the twelfth century. The south aisle was added late in the following century, and the north aisle was built sometime in the mid fourteenth century. Both aisles have decorative battlements and monstrous gargoyles. The capitals of the columns in the north aisle are noteworthy, with angels on one and characters from the *Roman de Renart* on the other — Reynard the fox running off with

a goose in his mouth, Cointereau the monkey with a chain and weight around his neck, Grimbert the badger and Noble the lion. The manor was held for several centuries by the Digby family and two of their monuments remain: Sir John (died 1269) in a coat of mail with his wife, and Sir Everard (died 1509). The font is Norman, the triple sedilia and piscina Decorated and the communion rail Georgian.

Twycross: St James.

The church is mainly fourteenth-century, restored in 1840 when the west gallery, organ and reredos were put in. The family pew of Earl Howe, complete with fireplace, is late eighteenth-century. The glory of this church is its twelfth- and thirteenth-century French stained glass, which was presented to William IV, who gave it to Earl Howe of nearby Gopsall Hall. Much of the glass in the east window came from the Sainte-Chapelle in Paris, with some from Saint-Denis, Saint-Julien-du-Sault and Le Mans Cathedral. Especially fine are the Presentation in the Temple and the Deposition from the Cross.

Wistow: St Wistan.

This church shares its unusual dedication with its near neighbour at Wigston. Wistan was a Christian prince of Mercia, murdered by his wicked uncle Brifardus. It seems likely that this was the site of his martyrdom. The church was remodelled in 1746 and so appears largely Georgian, but a blocked doorway to the right of the porch proclaims its Norman origin. The tower is late fifteenth-century. Inside, all the fittings date from the mid eighteenth century — plaster ceiling, pulpit, box pews, reredos and ironwork communion rails. The Halford family bought Wistow Hall in 1603 and the last member died in 1896, a remarkable span. Their monuments may be seen in the north chapel: Sir Richard (died 1658) reclining between two kneeling children, Sir William (died 1768) and three by R. Westmacott junior to Sir Henry (died 1844), physician to George III, George IV and William IV, his wife (died 1831) and Sir John Vaughan (died 1839).

The ruins of the castle at Ashby de la Zouch, with the church of St Helen, in the background.

Historic buildings and gardens

Ashby de la Zouch Castle, Ashby de la Zouch. Telephone: 0530 413343. English Heritage.

It was the Beaumont family, Earls of Leicester, who began to build a castle at Ashby, but before long it passed into the hands of the la Zouch family, in about 1160. Its most notable owner was William, Lord Hastings, who was granted the manor in 1464 by Edward IV and authorised to fortify it ten years later. This show of strength did not save him, however, for he was beheaded in 1483 by Richard III. His grandson was a loyal henchman of Henry VIII and was rewarded with the title of Earl of Huntingdon. The family retained their royal connections and Mary, Queen of Scots, James I and Charles I were visitors to Ashby. In the Civil War it was the second son of the fifth Earl, Henry Hastings, who took a leading role in raising an army for the King, using Ashby as a base. The town was a vital Midlands position since both Leicester and Nottingham were strongly Parliamentarian. The castle held out against sporadic attacks and sieges but was forced to surrender in February 1646, three months before Charles I himself surrendered at Newark. The castle was partially destroyed two years later by Parliament to prevent it becoming a centre of revolt. After the Restoration the Earls of Huntingdon made their home at Castle Donington.

Fortunately the ruins of the castle are still substantial and the tower-house built by Lord Hastings in 1476 is most impressive: four

storeys high, it is nearly 90 feet (27 metres), with walls 9 feet (3 metres) thick. It is not the earliest part to survive for both the hall and buttery range are twelfth-century, though remodelled in the fourteenth century and again in the sixteenth. At the same time as the first alterations a solar was added to the north-east end of the hall, and slightly later a large kitchen to the south-west end of the buttery. The chapel and adjoining building, known as the 'priests' rooms', both date from the time of Lord Hastings.

Belvoir Castle, Grantham, Lincolnshire NG31 6BR. Telephone: 0476 870262.

Seen from a distance, set on a wooded hill, Belvoir looks the perfect castle and it is only as one gets nearer that it becomes apparent that it was not built until the first quarter of the nineteenth century. There has been a castle at Belvoir since the end of the eleventh century, when Robert de Todeni, standard-bearer to William the Conqueror, was granted land here. He was buried in the priory he founded nearby, and his coffin was discovered in the eighteenth century and brought into the castle chapel. The castle came by marriage into the de Ros family, who strengthened it in 1267. In the Wars of the Roses Lord Ros supported Henry VI, and when Edward IV came to the throne his lands were confiscated and Belvoir was given to Lord Hastings. The latter was unable to take the castle without a struggle, in which it was badly damaged. It was stripped of its lead roof, which was used in the building of Ashby de la Zouch Castle. On the accession of Henry VII Belvoir was restored to Edmund, Lord Ros, and on his death it came by marriage into the Manners family. Thomas Manners, first Earl of Rutland, set about rebuilding it in 1528 and the castle was finished in 1555. It was held by a Royalist garrison in the Civil War and besieged in 1645, surrendering after four months. It was demolished in 1649, but a new mansion was started in 1655, which took thirteen years to build. The third Duke was responsible for improvements about 1750 but in 1801 the fifth Duchess decided that something grander was needed. By 1816 the extensive alterations were all but complete when a fire destroyed the north and east wings. Undaunted, the Duchess carried on and the castle was finished in 1830. It is still in the hands of the same family and is the home of the tenth Duke of Rutland.

The many turrets and towers, the castellations of the parapets and the contrast between the yellow ironstone of the main building and the grey stone features give the castle a fairy-tale appearance. Entering through the main gates, one comes through a passage full of weapons into the Guardroom, with a further display of arms and armour, and the military note is continued since the castle houses the Regimental Museum of the 17th/21st Lancers. The Ballroom, like the Guardroom, has a medieval look, with pillars and vaulting based, it is said, on Lincoln Cathedral. Here, as elsewhere, hang many family portraits, amongst them one of Captain Lord Robert Manners, by Sir Joshua Reynolds. Leading off this room are the Chinese rooms, so called from their silk wall hangings and lacquered furniture. In complete contrast is the Elizabeth Saloon in Louis XIV style with large mirrors and white panelling, heavily decorated with gilt designs. The ceiling is lavishly painted with mythological characters. The Grand Dining Room is equally sumptuous but more restrained in its decor. Amongst the fine silver here is a huge punch bowl weighing 1979 ounces. The Picture Gallery has many fine exhibits, including a portrait of Henry VIII by Holbein, as well as a set of five of the 'seven sacraments' by Poussin, and a hunting scene by the local artist John Ferneley. The longest room in the castle is the Regent's Gallery where the predominant colours are red, white and gold. Here is displayed the magnificent set of Louis XVI Gobelins tapestries depicting the adventures of Don Quixote. Further tapestries are to be found in the chapel, but these are seventeenth-century English from the royal manufactory at Mortlake, London, and show events from the Acts of the Apostles. The picture over the altar is by Murillo. Other rooms are open to the public, including the kitchen and beer cellars. The gardens are well laid out and there are special events held on Sundays and bank holidays during the summer.

Donington le Heath Manor House, Donington le Heath, Coalville. Telephone: 0530 31259. Leicestershire Museums Service.

Belvoir Castle, with its many turrets, seen from the air.

Donington le Heath Manor House.

The west tower, Kirby Muxloe Castle.

This small manor house dates from the late thirteenth century, with slight seventeenth-century alterations, mainly to the windows. It consists of two large rooms — the hall on the upper storey and the kitchen below — with two small wings on the north side. The house was inhabited until the 1960s and has now been restored by the county council, which has placed period furniture in the rooms and has laid out the garden.

Kirby Muxloe Castle, Kirby Muxloe, Leicester. Telephone: 0533 386886. English Heritage.

The Hastings family not only built Ashby de la Zouch Castle and played a part in the history of Belvoir Castle but were also responsible for fortifying Kirby Muxloe. They inherited the manor in the mid fourteenth century and may well have built the original moated manor house at that time. The ground plan of this house — hall, solar and kitchen — can be seen within the present castle. The same Lord Hastings who built Ashby Castle obtained permission to build at Kirby and work started in 1480. The plan was for an oblong building with a large central courtyard. The gatehouse is in the centre of the north-west wall, guarding the bridge across the moat, and the hall and kitchen were opposite (the original manor house was to have been demolished when the new building was complete). The whole building was in brick with stone dressings. At each corner of the castle three-storey towers were planned, but with Hastings's death in 1483 the work ground to a halt and the castle was never finished. As frequently happened with deserted buildings, the castle was dismantled gradually as brick and stone were removed for re-use elsewhere.

Only two parts of the castle remain standing to any height. The gatehouse is still very imposing with octagonal turrets at the corners, the outer ones having openings for cannon. The west tower is better preserved and is three storeys high with a turret that is higher still. It retains its battlements and was perhaps one of the few parts of the castle to be finished completely. Apart from a small section of wall near the gatehouse the rest of the building is reduced almost to ground level.

Leicester University Botanic Garden, Beaumont Hall, Stoughton Drive South, Oadby, Leicester LE2 2NA. Telephone: 0533 717725.

The gardens have been set out in the grounds of four large houses built early in the twentieth century and now used as student halls of residence. The gardens cover 16 acres (6.5 ha) and include an arboretum, heather garden, rock garden, water garden, woodland, herbaceous borders and specialised collections of, amongst others, roses and fuchsias. There are also glasshouses and plants are sometimes available for sale.

Lyddington Bede House, Bluecoat Lane, Lyddington, Oakham, Rutland. Telephone: 057282 2438. English Heritage.

The Bede House gets its name from its use as an almshouse from 1602. It was originally a palace belonging to the Bishops of Lincoln, who owned a house and parkland here from the beginning of the thirteenth century. The present building was built in the second quarter of the fifteenth century and altered towards the end of that century; the eastern part is an extension of 1767 in the same style. It used to be part of a range of buildings crossing the high end of the Great Hall of the palace, which ran off to the north.

The ground floor was the domestic quarters, now separated into smaller rooms for the bedesmen. The upper floor was for the Bishop — his audience chamber and private chamber. Both have fifteenth-century glass in the windows and finely carved and panelled ceilings. The servants' quarters were above. In the grounds, at the south-west corner of the gardens is a delightful octagonal stone summer-house with a pointed roof.

Oakham Castle, Oakham, Rutland. Enquiries to Rutland County Museum (see chapter 6). Telephone: 0572 723654. Leicestershire Museums Service.

In 1086 a castle was first recorded at Oakham. This would have been of timber and was replaced in about 1180-90 by the exceptionally fine stone hall that is still standing. It was built for Walkelin de Ferrers by the same masons who worked on the choir of Canter-

Lyddington Bede House.

Stanford Hall and stable block.

bury Cathedral. There is no documentary evidence for this but the carvings both inside and outside are so strikingly similar in design that this is a safe assumption.

The ramparts remain on three sides, with some of the stone wall still left. On the fourth side, the south, is the thirteenth-century gateway, much restored in 1872. The hall of the castle has also undergone some alteration but nonetheless is the earliest to survive so completely. It is rather like the nave of a church with a north and south aisle. Inside, the west end is still arranged as a court, but it is the horseshoes hanging on the walls that first attract the eye. There is an ancient custom that any peer of the realm visiting Oakham for the first time must pay homage to the Lord of the Manor by presenting a horseshoe. The earliest attributable shoe is mid to late fifteenth-century and some of the most recent have been given by members of the Royal Family.

Stanford Hall, Stanford, Lutterworth LE17 6DH. Telephone: 0788 860250.

The present owners of Stanford Hall are direct descendants of Peter Cave, who first came to Stanford as a tenant of Selby Abbey in 1430. At the Dissolution of the Monasteries the manor was bought by his great-grandson Sir Thomas Cave. The old manor house was, like the church and the village, on the Northamptonshire side of the river Avon. In 1697 Sir

Roger Cave commissioned William Smith of Warwick to demolish the old house and to build a new one on the Leicestershire side of the river. He died in 1703 before it was completed, and his son, Sir Thomas, moved in the following year. The east front of the house was rebuilt in a more imposing style in about 1735, and the saloon and grand staircase were remodelled in 1745. Since then, apart from some slight alterations during the restoration of 1880, the house has changed very little. Electric lighting was installed in the 1890s without taking up the floorboards, by the cunning use of ferrets. A hole was made at each end of the room and a ferret with flex attached to its collar was put in one hole and rapidly made its way towards the other hole, where a piece of rabbit was dangled as bait.

The exterior of the house is pleasing — the somewhat conservative grey stone south front is balanced by the more formal Palladian style of the brick east front. Close by is the equally elegant stable block, which dates from 1737. Most of the ground-floor rooms of the house and two of the bedrooms can be visited.

There is beautiful panelling and fine plasterwork on the ceilings, notably in the ballroom. Hung on the walls are many portraits of members of the family and royalty, including pictures by Kneller and van Dyck. In particular there are a number of relics of the Stuarts bought by Baroness Braye, who happened to be in Rome when the effects of the last of the family, Henry, Cardinal Duke of York, were sold after his death. There is also some good furniture, tapestries and interesting documents, including the accounts for the building of the house. In the grounds are a walled rose garden, a nature trail and a replica of the flying machine that Percy Pilcher used for his fatal flight in 1899. The Stanford Hall Motorcycle Museum is described in chapter 6.

Tolethorpe Hall, Little Casterton, Stamford, Lincolnshire. Telephone: 0780 54381.

The manor house is medieval in origin but was rebuilt at the end of the sixteenth century, enlarged in the seventeenth and 'restored' in 1867. The exterior has not suffered too much and still appears Jacobean but the interior has been almost completely altered. Its main claim to fame is that it is the birthplace of Robert Browne, who in 1581 broke away from the Church of England to form a congregationalist sect which lived on well into the seventeenth

century, some followers being executed for treason by Elizabeth I. Browne himself returned to being an Anglican vicar in 1585. Tolethorpe Hall is now the home of the Stamford Shakespeare Company, which annually presents three plays during the summer months in an outdoor auditorium. The grounds are open at weekends in the summer.

Whatton Gardens, Long Whatton, Loughborough. Telephone: 0509 842302.

The gardens of Whatton House cover about 25 acres (10 ha) in all. The most unusual part is probably the Chinese Garden, which is laid out with a variety of bronze ornaments, pagodas and arches. There are formal and wilderness areas — shrub and herbaceous borders, heathers, rock pools with fish, rose gardens, an arboretum with a fine selection of mature trees and a kitchen garden of the same date as the house (about 1802). Various follies and summerhouses are sited around the grounds.

The horseshoes in Oakham Castle.

6
Museums

ASHBY DE LA ZOUCH

Ashby de la Zouch Museum, 13-15 Lower Church Street, Ashby de la Zouch LE6 5AB. Telephone: 0530 415603.

There is a particular emphasis in this small museum on the history and role of the castle and the Hastings family. Other varied displays are devoted to items of local interest.

CASTLE DONINGTON

The Donington Collection, Donington Park, Castle Donington, Derby DE7 2RP. Telephone: 0332 810048.

This museum is a mecca for motor-racing enthusiasts as it is the largest collection of single-seater racing cars in the world. There are over 150 cars on display, from Alfa Romeos to a Wolf Cosworth, with a host of famous marques in between. Also exhibited are Mike Hailwood's and Barry Sheene's collections of racing motorcycles. There is a speedway Hall of Fame.

East Midlands Aeropark and Visitor Centre, East Midlands International Airport, Castle Donington, Derby DE7 2SA. Telephone: 0332 810621 extension 3361.

The aim of the centre is to give a brief history of the airport, together with a large-scale model, and the history of flight in general and civil aviation in particular. This is done by a video presentation, aircraft models and parts, including jet engines. Outside in the Aeropark are several aircraft, amongst them a Vickers Varsity, an Avro Vulcan bomber and a Westland Whirlwind helicopter. From the nearby viewing mound spectators can see the commercial aircraft landing and taking off at close quarters.

LEICESTER

Belgrave Hall, Church Road, Belgrave, Leicester LE4 5PE. Telephone: 0533 669413.

Belgrave, now a suburb largely of terraced houses, was once a pleasant little village. On turning off Thurcaston Road into Church Road, however, one is immediately away from the sprawl of Leicester. On either side of the road leading to the church, which is mainly of the thirteenth and fourteenth centuries, are two fine red-brick houses of the eighteenth century. On the right is Belgrave House, built in classical style in 1776, and on the left the earlier Belgrave Hall in Queen Anne style of 1713. Both are owned by the Museums Service, the former used for conservation and storage and the latter open to the public.

Belgrave Hall has been furnished in keeping with its period and gives an insight into daily life of times past. The entrance hall is wide and has a door at the back leading straight into the garden. The ground-floor rooms are the dining room, drawing room with a good red lacquer bureau, and the kitchen. Unusually this is at the front of the house, which seems to be its original position. The kitchen is one of the most interesting rooms, with a variety of utensils, some familiar and others which have long been superseded. Upstairs are the bedrooms, each furnished in a different style, and the music room complete with instruments, including a harp of 1826 and a square piano of about 1790.

Outside in the stable block is the heavy coach made in 1740 for the Herrick family of Beaumanor, which dwarfs the Victorian brougham that was once at Baggrave Hall. There are also all sorts of agricultural implements, and a dairy with all the things necessary for cheese-making, even cheese presses of Swithland slate. The succession of walled gardens is very attractive, some laid out in period style, others as a rock garden, water garden or botanical garden. Part of the garden was across the road in front of the house. This is now a park, Belgrave Gardens.

The Guildhall, Guildhall Lane, Leicester LE1 5FQ. Telephone: 0533 532569.

In 1343 the Corpus Christi Guild was founded as a lay religious body attached to St Martin's church and before very long built a meeting place for itself adjacent to the church. The Guild quickly became a powerful force in local affairs, and its two Masters even took precedence over the Mayor of the town. The Corporation, having no permanent building of its own, used the Guildhall and took it over when the Guild was dissolved at the Reformation. It remained the headquarters of the Town Council until the Town Hall was built in 1876.

The oldest part of the building is the east end of the Great Hall, which dates from about 1350 and uses large curved timbers known as crucks to support the roof. The west end of the hall is later, about 1490, and uses the post and truss system. At the same time the west wing was built. This was converted into a two-storey building in 1563 when the ground floor became the Mayor's Parlour. The panelling and richly carved overmantel date from 1637, as do the Mayor's chair and the fine royal arms above it. Some of the original stained glass remains in the windows. The east wing may have been the living quarters of the chantry priests who served the Corpus Christi Guild. It was remodelled in 1632 when the Town Library, which

The interior of the Guildhall, Leicester, looking west, showing the two methods of construction.

had been housed in the belfry of St Martins was installed in the upper floor. In the Library may be seen the huge Beaumanor Chair, made in 1690 from the trunk of an oak tree that was blown down in a gale. Squeezed in between the Library and the Great Hall is a tiny room furnished as the Recorder's Bedroom. The ground floor of the east wing was converted into cells when the Guildhall also became the Police Station in 1840. The south wing, which had been the banqueting kitchens, was demolished in 1836 to be replaced by the Constable's House. In the Police Station are exhibited truncheons, thumb screws, a scold's bridle, handcuffs, leg-irons and gibbet-irons, in which the bodies of hanged criminals were displayed as a warning to others. One of the cells has also been furnished as it would have been early in the nineteenth century.

The Jewry Wall Museum, St Nicholas Circle, Leicester LE1 4LB. Telephone: 0533 544766.

With its proximity to the Roman Baths and Jewry Wall one would expect this museum to have a bias towards Roman Leicester, but the exhibits cover the whole period from prehistoric times through to the middle ages. It is impossible to do justice to such a large time scale within the confines of such a small

gallery, so the emphasis is on daily life and death. Scale models are used to good effect — particularly striking is the half-size Celtic chariot. There are stone age and iron age tools and querns for milling wheat that were found at Breedon on the Hill. Roman decorative work is well represented with wall paintings and mosaics. The most interesting of these is perhaps the small Cyparissus pavement, which depicts a youth leaning against a stag accompanied by a cupid, but the other two are more impressive by virtue of their size. Each originally measured some 20 feet (6 metres) square but neither is now complete. Both are dated to the middle of the second century AD and consist of nine octagonal panels of floral and geometric design. The centrepiece of one is a peacock displaying his spread tail. Death looms large with a Roman coffin and skeleton. An Anglo-Saxon skeleton, laid out with funeral objects that would be needed in the next world, is accompanied by a reconstruction clothed as authentically as possible and decorated with replicas of the jewellery found with the skeleton. A different Anglo-Saxon burial practice is evidenced by the cremation urns that were discovered at Thurmaston. The major exhibit from the middle ages is the glass from Wygston's House, which shows the

Left: *The Peacock mosaic in the Jewry Wall Museum, Leicester.*
Right: *The Resurrection: early sixteenth-century stained glass from Wygston's House, now in the Jewry Wall Museum, Leicester.*

Seven Sacraments of the Church, the Seven Corporal Acts of Mercy and the Life and Joys of the Virgin Mary.

John Doran Gas Museum, Aylestone Road, Leicester LE2 7QH. Telephone: 0533 549414, extension 2192.

The museum is located in the gatehouse of what was Leicester Corporation's gasworks, now the Leicester Service Centre. This was built in 1878, together with its impressive clock tower and the fine terrace of houses for the gasworkers. The museum aims to demonstrate how gas was made and used. Of more general interest is the collection of gas lights and domestic appliances, including fires and cookers, notably one of about 1930 which has a blue and white willow pattern design on its splash-back and oven door. In addition, however, are washing machines, irons, hairdryers, magic lanterns and a gas wireless of 1939.

The Leicestershire Museum and Art Gallery, New Walk, Leicester LE1 6TD. Telephone: 0533 554100.

The museum building originated as a school for nonconformists in 1836 but assumed its present use in 1849. The grand portico suggests an important building though architecturally it is remarkably dull. The architect was J. A. Hansom, better known as the inventor of the hansom cab. The interior was modernised in 1975 and only the picture gallery, which doubles as a concert room, retains any feel of its Victorian past. This houses a representative collection of nineteenth-century British paintings, including works by Lord Leighton, G. F. Watts and William Dyce. Their larger-than-life classical and biblical compositions are contrasted with Frith's 'The Railway Station', which is packed full of everyday detail as passengers board a train at Paddington Station. Also hung here are sporting pictures by Herring and Ferneley (see the Melton Carnegie Museum for more of his work).

Notable Old Master paintings are 'The Choirboy' by Georges de la Tour and 'The Holy Family with St John' by Poussin. Eight-

28

eenth-century British art includes works by Hogarth and Gainsborough and a charming picture by Thomas Hudson of 'Mrs Matthew Michell and Her Children', dated 1757-8, in which her young son holds an early cricket bat and ball. The Leicester celebrity Daniel Lambert (see chapter 9) is the subject of a painting by Ben Marshall, himself a Leicestershire man born at Seagrave in 1768. Among twentieth-century works are paintings by Lowry, Stanley Spencer and Graham Sutherland. The collection of German Impressionist and Expressionist art is particularly fine, and the sculpture collection is also noteworthy. Glass, ceramics and silver complete the fine art displays.

The Ancient Egyptian exhibits are of interest, particularly to children, who enjoy the painted coffins complete with mummies in side, and the mummified cat and hawks. Faience and bronze amulets and grave ornaments are on display, and images of the gods to explain the religious beliefs of the time.

The remainder of the museum is devoted to prehistory and natural history, especially birds. Towering above all is the Rutland dinosaur: a brontosaurus skeleton found at Great Casterton in 1968. Even though half of it is a reconstruction, it is still one of the most complete ever discovered. Other remains

come from limestone quarries at Barrow upon Soar and are of ichthyosaurs and a plesiosaur.

The Leicestershire Museum of Technology, Abbey Pumping Station, Corporation Road, Leicester LE4 5PW. Telephone: 0533 661330.

These buildings were once the Abbey Sewage Pumping Station, and pride of place in the collection must go to the four steam beam engines of 1891, still *in situ*. They are immaculately decorated and are housed in a splendid engine room with cast-iron Corinthian columns. An earlier A-frame beam engine of 1826 is also exhibited in the adjoining hall, where most of the items on display are concerned with transport. There is a collection of early bicycles, including a penny-farthing and two bone shakers, one of which was made in Leicester. Early motor bicycles are also featured. There are delivery vehicles, a hearse and a horse-drawn steam fire-engine. The museum collection of transport contains old buses and lorries, but these are brought out for the public only at special events. In the grounds is a large steam shovel of 1935. Since one of the major industries in Leicestershire is hosiery and knitwear it is not surprising to find a range of knitting machines from the eighteenth century to the modern domestic variety.

The beam engines in the Leicestershire Museum of Technology, Leicester.

Museum of the Royal Leicestershire Regiment, The Magazine, Oxford Street, Leicester. Telephone: 0533 555889.

It is fitting that the regimental museum should be situated in this building, which has been used by the military since the Civil War. It was built as the main gateway to the Newarke in about 1410, but the arch through the three-storey tower now leads nowhere as a dual carriageway passes either side and the museum can be reached only by a pedestrian subway. Inside are items illustrating the history of the Royal Leicestershire Regiment from its formation in 1688 until its absorption into the Royal Anglian Regiment. There are uniforms, weapons, medals, including several Victoria Crosses, a fine display of regimental silver, an eighteenth-century serpent and a variety of campaign souvenirs such as a Burmese temple bell and captured machine guns from the First World War.

Newarke Houses Museum, The Newarke, Leicester LE2 7BY. Telephone: 0533 554100.

The Museum of Social History is housed in two buildings now interconnected. Both are of sixteenth-century origin, but so rebuilt since then that from the outside they appear to be early nineteenth-century. Inside, too, there have been alterations. Several rooms have been panelled — that to the right of the entrance hall is about 1650, and the room has been furnished with largely contemporary items, apart from a splendid suit of armour from Augsburg dating from 1520-40. The room to the left has eighteenth-century panelling but the furniture is all by Ernest Gimson, born in Leicester in 1864. He was one of the leading lights of the Arts and Crafts Movement until his death in 1919. Particularly striking are his inlaid boxes and cabinets, but the simplicity of his rush-seated chairs is also very effective. The other notable room is upstairs where both the panelling and the overmantel are dated 1651 and come from Ragdale Hall. In this room is some of the stained glass from Wygston's House.

The exhibits are changed from time to time but certain items are on permanent display. These include Daniel Lambert's clothes and chairs (see chapter 9) and a fine collection of long-case and lantern clocks. A nineteenth-century street scene has been reconstructed with several shop-fronts and a cobbler's workshop, a framework knitter and watchmaker's workshop. The latter is especially interesting as all the items belonged originally to Samuel Deacon, who set up his shop at Barton in the Beans near Market Bosworth in 1771. The workshop remained unchanged until one of his descendants sold the family home in 1951, when all the contents were brought to the museum. There are also displays of domestic gadgets, homecrafts and a 1940s village shop. Harassed parents bringing children to the museum will find that there is always one room with a display of toys, some antique but others definitely within living memory!

Wygston's House Museum of Costume, 12 Applegate, St Nicholas Circle, Leicester LE1 5LD. Telephone: 0533 554100.

The museum gets its name from the original owner of the house, Roger Wyggeston, who died in 1509. The central portion of the building is a timber-framed hall of about 1480 with an upper storey projecting on brackets. It would have had cross-wings at either end, but these have been replaced at the rear by a nineteenth-century brick building and at the front, facing the road, by a fine three-storey building of the late eighteenth century. This front part houses the displays of costume from the eighteenth to the twentieth centuries, mostly arranged in family groupings with contemporary furnishings in the rooms. The central section is used for exhibitions and the rear has been reconstructed as examples of shops of the 1920s. One is a shoe shop and the other a draper's. Particularly interesting is the 'cash railway', a means of getting money from the counter to the cashier by putting it into a hollow ball and rolling it along a track suspended from the ceiling. The stained glass of about 1500 that was once in the ground floor windows is now in the Newarke Houses and Jewry Wall Museums.

LOUGHBOROUGH

The Bell Foundry Museum, Freehold Street, Loughborough LE11 1AR. Telephone: 0509 233414.

This unique museum is devoted to bells and their manufacture and is situated in the former fettling shop of the foundry. Bells have been cast in Loughborough since John Taylor came to the town in 1839 to recast the bells of the parish church. His father had cast bells in Oxford since 1821, and it was decided to establish a branch at Loughborough. Taylors' links can be traced back much further than that — right to the fourteenth century when John de Stafford, a bellfounder, was Mayor of Leicester. It is from this early period that the evolution of bellfounding is traced, showing the moulding, casting, tuning and final fitting up of the bells. Taylors were responsible for casting the heaviest bell in Britain, 'Great Paul', for St Paul's Cathedral, London, in 1881. It weighs 37,483 pounds (17,002 kg) and it was quite a feat transporting it to its destination. Bells are still cast in the adjoining foundry and guided tours for parties of visitors can be made by prior arrangement.

The tuning room at Taylors' Bellfoundry, Loughborough.

The Old Rectory Museum, Steeple Row, Loughborough LE11 1UX. Telephone: 0509 214995. Charnwood Borough Council.

The Old Rectory is the remains of a fourteenth-century building with a ruined hall and adjacent two-storey wing. It was the home of the rectors of the parish until 1958, though much rebuilt over the centuries. All the later additions were demolished in 1962, leaving the medieval core, which is now cared for by the Loughborough and District Archaeological Society. They exhibit items of local interest, some of which have been discovered in the course of their excavations. These include ridge tiles from the medieval moated manor site at Long Whatton and floor tiles from Garendon Abbey, decorated with a butterfly, an alphabet in reverse, birds and other motifs. There is also an interesting gravestone to Sarah Johnson, who died in 1819 at the age of 28. She suffered from ascites (dropsy) and fluid was drained from her 28 times, the amount taken on each occasion being carefully recorded on the stone. It totalled 310 gallons 1 quart 1 pint (1411 litres).

MARKET HARBOROUGH

The Harborough Museum, Council Offices, Adam and Eve Street, Market Harborough LE16 7LT. Telephone: 0858 32468.

As befits a museum housed in a former corset factory, the Harborough Museum has an intimate atmosphere. It has items relating both to the town's history and also to the present day, highlighted by a reconstructed shoemaker's workroom, in use from 1901 to 1986. There are displays tracing the development of the town from its trading origins in the twelfth century to its importance as a coaching stop in the eighteenth, and as a manufacturing centre in the nineteenth. Much of the space is devoted to special exhibitions, often of local interest.

MELTON MOWBRAY

Melton Carnegie Museum, Thorpe End, Melton Mowbray LE13 1RB. Telephone: 0664 69946.

The museum houses mainly exhibits of local interest with an emphasis on making pork pies and Stilton cheese (see chapter 10), though it includes such curiosities as a two-headed calf. Of national importance, however, is the work of John Ferneley, born at Thrussington in 1782. He spent some time studying with Ben Marshall in London and moved around for a few years before settling at Melton in 1814. Here he was well placed to paint the sporting pictures for which he is famous as the town was full of wealthy patrons who were keen foxhunters. A good example of his art is the group portrait of John, Henry and Francis Grant at

'John, Henry and Francis Grant', by John Ferneley, in the Melton Carnegie Museum, Melton Mowbray.

Melton, dated 1823, which is on display. Of more human interest, however, is his unfinished painting of 'The Ferneley Family Pew in Melton Church', painted between 1821 and 1826. None of his children appears to be paying the slightest attention to the preacher!

NORMANTON

Normanton Church Water Museum, Whitwell Manor, Rutland Water, Oakham, Rutland LE15 8BW. Telephone: 078086 321. Anglian Water.

The village of Normanton was levelled in 1764 when Sir Gilbert Heathcote decided to extend the parkland of Normanton Hall. At the same time he rebuilt the church, leaving the medieval tower intact. That was replaced by the present west end in 1826, the nave and chancel being rebuilt in a style to match in 1911. The hall was demolished in 1925, leaving only the church, and now that is surrounded by Rutland Water. It has become a local landmark — somewhat resembling a toy steamer floating on the reservoir — protected from the water and linked to the shore by an embankment. It was deconsecrated in 1970 and began its new life as a museum in 1984. Inside is an exhibition relating to the history and work of Anglian Water, and also to the local history of the area. On show is a well preserved Anglo-Saxon skeleton, unearthed during the construction of the reservoir.

OAKHAM

Rutland County Museum, Catmos Street, Oakham, Rutland LE15 6HW. Telephone: 0572 723654.

The museum is housed in what was the Riding School of the Rutland Fencible Cavalry, built in 1795, and the adjoining building, which was the Poultry Hall of the Rutland Agricultural Society. The main emphasis of the museum is rural. In the yard there are vintage tractors, carts, wagons, ploughs and a threshing machine, as well as the game larder. Inside are varying displays of seed drills, handcarts and tools used by tradesmen such as blacksmiths, coopers and wheelwrights. There are domestic bygones and exhibits relating to the geology and archaeology of Rutland, including bronze axe-heads and Anglo-Saxon brooches and clasps. One gallery is devoted to the history of the Leicestershire Yeomanry and Volunteer Regiments.

Rutland Farm Park, Catmose Farm, Uppingham Road, Oakham, Rutland LE15 6JD. Telephone: 0572 56789.

This farm once formed part of the Catmose Estate and the farm buildings date back to the 1830s. There are mature trees on the 18 acre (7 ha) site, notably oak, ash, yew, walnut and wellingtonia. A wooded area contains a stream, magnificent stands of bamboo and many unusual ferns; more than sixty bird species have been recorded. There is a wild-flower meadow and a small cereal plot.

Another attraction is the unusual farm livestock. Among the many breeds are shaggy Highland, ancient White Park and Old English Longhorn cattle. The Manx Loghtan sheep, with fine brown fleeces and large horns, were introduced to the Isle of Man by the Vikings. The Soay sheep are also of historical interest as they are the descendants of the flocks first domesticated in prehistoric times. As well as other breeds of cattle, sheep, pigs and poultry, the Farm Park has a small herd of Bagot and Old English goats, Shetland ponies and a fine herd of Exmoor ponies. A wide variety of old tractors, horse-drawn vehicles, agricultural implements and hand tools is on display to give an understanding of what farming was like in the nineteenth and early twentieth centuries.

STANFORD

Stanford Hall Motorcycle Museum, Lutterworth LE17 6DH. Telephone: 0788 860250.

In the grounds of Stanford Hall is a very fine collection of vintage motorcycles and three-wheeler cars. Since the majority of vehicles are lent by private owners the exhibits are changed frequently. Most Sundays during the summer there are car and motorcycle rallies organised by a variety of owners' clubs.

A Saxon cruciform brooch from Empingham, now in the Rutland County Museum, Oakham.

The packhorse bridge at Anstey.

7
Industrial archaeology

Leicestershire is often regarded as a comparatively rural county, so it comes as a surprise to many to discover that coal has been mined in the Swannington area since at least the thirteenth century, and that iron ore, granite and Swithland slate have been quarried since Roman times and probably earlier. Even the rural nature of the east of the county has its own industry, not only in the picturesque windmills but also in the wool trade. This has now largely been supplanted by the hosiery industry. The first knitting frame was installed in Hinckley some time before 1640, but it was not until the nineteenth century that Leicestershire became the centre of the hosiery trade, despite the attacks on the improved machinery by the Luddites, named, it is said, after Ned Ludd of Anstey. The boot and shoe industry was a relative latecomer amongst Leicestershire industries but it flourished from the 1850s. The late eighteenth and the nineteenth centuries also saw a great improvement in transport, with the building of canals and railways to further trade by opening up new markets. In the late twentieth century a wide variety of mainly light industry provides employment for the people of Leicestershire. Fortunately traces of earlier commercial and industrial activity survive and are being preserved for future generations.

Anstey Packhorse Bridge, Leicester Road, Anstey, Leicester (OS 140: SK 552085).

Just beside the modern bridge into Anstey on the road from Leicester is a packhorse bridge of five arches, 54 feet (16.5 metres) long and 5 feet (1.5 metres) wide between the parapets. The date is disputed but it is no later than the seventeenth century; indeed it is possible that it was built about 1500 by the Greys to ease the journey from Bradgate to Leicester.

Arnesby Windmill, Arnesby, Leicester (OS 140: SP 615925).

The present tower mill was built in 1815, perhaps on the base of an earlier post mill, and continued working until about 1914. Thereafter it was left to decay until 1976, when it was restored to something like its original external appearance and a house was built alongside. It is not in working order.

Aylestone Packhorse Bridge, Marsden Lane, Aylestone, Leicester (OS 140: SK 566009).

There is much transport history very close together in this part of the Soar valley. Approaching the packhorse bridge from Aylestone, one first goes under a bridge which carried the Great Central Railway and over a bridge beneath which flows the Grand Union

Canal at its junction with the river Soar. The packhorse bridge was built in the fifteenth century for the benefit of the growing coal trade between Swannington and Leicester, and has eight arches and three refuges or passing points.

Claybrooke Mill, Frolesworth Lane, Claybrooke Magna, Lutterworth LE17 5DB (OS 140: SP 499891). Telephone: 0455 202443.

This watermill, on a tributary of the river Soar, has been restored and started grinding flour again in 1988, having previously ceased production 25 years before. The present three-storey building, which houses an internal overshot wooden wheel, dates from the eighteenth century, but there has been a mill on this site since the thirteenth century. Visits may be made by appointment.

Foxton Locks, Gumley Road, Foxton, Market Harborough (OS 141: SP 691897). Leicestershire County Council. Car park on the Gumley road ½ mile south-west of Foxton.

In the late eighteenth century, at the height of the canal boom, there was an ambitious project to enable barges using the Trent and Soar to link into the canal network and so reach London. This meant building a canal from Leicester through the south of the county to join the Grand Junction Canal in Northamptonshire. By 1797 the Leicestershire and Northamptonshire Union Canal had reached Debdale Wharf near Kibworth but was forced to stop because of shortage of funds and the opposition of Sir John Palmer of Foxton. It was decided to avoid Foxton and when work began again the canal was re-routed to Market Harborough. This section was finished in 1809. The Grand Junction Canal then took up the project, reverting to the original idea of taking the canal up the hill at Foxton and across to Long Buckby in Northamptonshire. To do this required a flight of locks to climb the 75 foot (23 metre) slope. Finance was still a problem, so the locks were built wide enough for only one barge at a time, though there is a passing pond between the two five-lock 'staircases'. The locks were completed in 1812 and the section to Long Buckby finally opened in 1814. There must always have been a bottleneck here for trade quickly prospered, with coal, stone and farming produce going to London and manufactured goods coming back. In the second half of the nineteenth century the canals came under increased competition from the railways and in a final effort to overcome the congestion and delay a barge lift was installed in 1900. This comprised two large counterbalanced water tanks capable of taking two barges each, which ran on tracks up and down an inclined plane. It was used for only ten years before it became uneconomic owing to the decline in traffic on the canal.

Foxton Locks are a favourite attraction for visitors and are very picturesque. In addition to the flight of locks and inclined plane there are lock-keeper's cottages at the top and bottom of the locks, together with associated canal company buildings, and three fine brick bridges. There are regular barge trips on the canal.

John o'Gaunt Viaduct, Twyford, Melton Mowbray (OS 141: SK 741092).

The Great Northern and London and North Western Joint Railway built a line from Melton Mowbray to Market Harborough in 1878-9 and in so doing erected this brick-built viaduct of fourteen arches across a valley and narrow stream.

Kibworth Harcourt Windmill, Langton Road, Kibworth Harcourt, Leicester (OS 141: SP 689944).

This mill is unique in the county, being the only remaining post mill and the only mill complete with sails and machinery. It was built in the seventeenth century and has four sails. The two-storey wooden body is built on a brick roundhouse and is turned by a tailpole.

Leicester's industrial heritage

Leicester has two museums devoted to industrial items — the John Doran Gas

The flight of locks on the Grand Union Canal at Foxton.

Museum and the Museum of Technology (see chapter 6) — but in addition there are many buildings and other things to see. The largest and most impressive is the only passenger station still in use in the city, **London Road Station.** It was built for the Midland Railway Company in 1892, replacing their earlier station of 1840, built in the classical style. The fine exterior is of brick with stone dressings and terracotta decorations and has a domed clock-tower at the northern corner. The interior of the building and the platforms have been thoroughly modernised. The other surviving station, the **Central Station** in Great Central Street, was built in a similar style in 1899, but no longer serves its original purpose and its facade has been shorn of its shaped gables and clock-tower. The gateway to the parcels offices still retains its bold inscription.

It is possible to walk along the banks of the river Soar and the Grand Union Canal throughout their length in the city. From the eastern corner of Abbey Park one can see **Lime Kiln Lock** and, on the opposite bank, **Memory Lane Wharf,** which used to be a centre for passenger traffic on the canal. Following either the canal or the river southwest, one comes to Frog Island. The building to note here is **Martin's Dyeworks,** built in 1874 as a spinning mill. It is in a classical style with a pediment on the facade and interesting brickwork. Walking south, one rejoins the canal at **North Lock** and goes south-west, meeting the river at Hitchcock's Weir and again at Evans' Weir. Further along, on the opposite bank, is the factory of **Donisthorpe and Company Limited**, which is readily recognisable by the cupola on the roof which once held a bell which was rung as a flood warning. This four-storey pedimented building dates from the late eighteenth or early nineteenth century and was originally a worsted spinning mill. The front of the factory on Sarah Street is less interesting. Near the **West Bridge** are two terracotta reliefs of mermaids, which once adorned the entrance arch of the now-demolished wholesale market in Halford Street. They were designed in Art Nouveau style by Neatby and made by Doulton in 1900. The West Bridge itself is an impressive iron-built structure of 1890-1. Just south of here on the west bank is **Peck's factory,** a five-storey building with an Italian-style tower, built as a worsted spinning mill by William Flint in 1840.

Another part of the city which is worth a visit is Rutland Street. The jewel here is **Alexandra House, number 47,** which is entirely faced in buff terracotta. It has a dome, turrets, spires, balconies and a mass of other ornamentation — all to house bootlaces and other ancillary items for the boot and shoe trade! It was designed by Burgess for Faire Brothers and was finished in 1898. Opposite is **number 78-80,** a belated Art Nouveau leather warehouse, built in 1923 for Pfister and Vogel. Finally, **number 29**, built in 1875 as a shoe and leather warehouse, has an Italianate yellow-brick facade, with stone medallions either side of the door depicting Mercury holding a sailing ship and Minerva with a steam engine.

Moira Furnace, Furnace Lane, Moira, Coalville (OS 128: SK 315152). North-West Leicestershire District Council.

Moira takes its rather unusual name from the Earl of Moira, who owned the land on which it was built. Both iron ore and coal were mined in the area, and it seemed logical to save on transport cost, and have a blast furnace here to extract iron from the ore. It was built in about 1804, around the same time as the completion of the adjacent Ashby de la Zouch Canal, which was cut from Bedworth on the Coventry Canal to the Ashby Woulds coalfield. It was used only intermittently as the coal was too good for use in smelting and the ore too poor to give sufficient iron. After only forty years or so it fell into disuse and the foundry and engine house were converted to cottages.

The furnace is one of the earliest to survive in so complete a state. Even so, the engine house was demolished as recently as 1974. This was where the Newcomen steam engine provided the blast of cold air to the furnace to

John o'Gaunt Viaduct.

Above: *Donisthorpe's factory, by the canal in Leicester.*

Below: *Moira Furnace. The molten iron ran out through the archway at the bottom into a bed of sand.*

keep the fire burning at the right temperature to smelt the ore. The coal and ore were fed into the furnace from the top and the molten iron at 2200 F (1200 C) was run off into the 'pig bed' at the bottom, through the arch which is now bricked up.

Moira Furnace is the centrepiece of the Moira Trail, devised by the Leicestershire Industrial History Society, who have produced an excellent leaflet describing eighteen points of interest in this locality. These include lime kilns, the line of a tramway, two railways, a weighing-machine house, another engine house and terraces of workers' houses.

Morcott Windmill, Barrowden Road, Morcott, Oakham, Rutland (OS 141: SK 931002).

There has probably been a mill on this site for centuries but the present tower mill was built early in the nineteenth century. Like many mills, it was working until the First World War but thereafter became derelict. It was reduced to a shell of two storeys and not restored until 1968, when it was rebuilt to four storeys, and cap, sails and fan were added.

Swannington Incline, Swannington, Leicester (OS 129: SK 420157).

The Leicestershire collieries were in difficulties after the failure of the Charnwood Forest Canal, which was never able to overcome its inherent problems; coal brought by canal from Nottinghamshire was cheaper in Leicester than coal carted from the west of the county.

In 1829 it was decided to ask Robert Stephenson to build a railway to transport the coal and the first steam-operated line in the Midlands — the Leicester and Swannington Railway — was opened in 1832. Several feats of engineering were required, including a tunnel at Glenfield, the longest then in existence, of 1796 yards (1642 metres), and an incline at

Morcott Windmill.

Bagworth. The incline at Swannington is, however, the most important.

The 1 in 17 gradient was too steep for steam locomotives, so a stationary steam engine, now in the National Railway Museum, York, was used to haul the wagons full of coal from the nearby Peggs Green, Califat and Calcutta collieries to the top of the incline. The locomotives took over at this point, hauling the coal to Leicester. When the mines were exhausted Calcutta was used as a pumping station to drain more distant mines and the incline was used to lower coal to the pump. The incline is being restored and is the main attraction of a trail which takes in other noteworthy sites including the tramway line at the end of the Charnwood Forest Canal, Califat and Calcutta mines, some early surface mines known as bell pits and Swannington windmill.

Welland Viaduct, Seaton, Oakham, Rutland. (OS 141: SP 914977).

The Midland Railway Company needed to build this viaduct to cross the Welland valley in 1876-8 and take trains down into Northamptonshire and on to London. It is the longest surviving viaduct in the county and certainly the most spectacular, being over ¾ mile (1 km) long, with 82 arches, each of 40 feet (12 metres) span, and 70 feet (21 metres) at its greatest height. Nearby Seaton station on the now dismantled London and North Western Railway is a good example of a station built to serve a small village.

Wymondham Windmill, Wymondham, Melton Mowbray LE14 2AD (OS 130: SK 850193). Telephone: 057284 584.

This is the only windmill in the county that is regularly open to visitors. It seems to have been built early in the nineteenth century and is unusual in that the five-storey tower is of ironstone and not the more common brick. All the machinery is intact but the six sails, removed after being damaged in a gale in 1922, have not yet been restored.

Welland Viaduct.

King Richard's Well at Bosworth Field.

8
Other places to visit

The Battlefield Line, Shackerstone Station, Shackerstone, Nuneaton, Warwickshire. Telephone: 0827 880754.

A steam-hauled passenger service runs 3 miles between Shackerstone and Market Bosworth. Plans are in hand to extend the line to Shenton, which is close to the site of the battle of Bosworth. The line was originally part of the Nuneaton and Ashby Joint Midland and London and North Western Railway line built in 1873. At Shackerstone station is a large collection of railway relics, as well as eight steam locomotives, several diesels and much rolling stock. The station building is typical of the period and was once used by King Edward VII on his way to Gopsall Hall.

Bosworth Battlefield Visitor Centre and Country Park, Sutton Cheney, Market Bosworth, Nuneaton, Warwickshire CV13 0AD. Telephone: 0455 290429.

On 22nd August 1485 the final battle of the Wars of the Roses took place between Richard III, the Yorkist King of England, and Henry Tudor, Earl of Richmond, of the Lancastrian line, resulting in Richard's death and Henry becoming Henry VII. It was a hard-fought battle and decided only by the intervention of Lord Stanley and his forces, who had waited on the sidelines until they could see which side was in the ascendancy. The events leading up to the battle and the fateful day itself are recounted at the visitor centre, using displays, models and maps to give as full an understanding as possible. The Battle Trail has been laid out around the site to show the strategy of that day and information boards describe the stages of the battle. Other footpaths are open and horse-drawn boat trips are available along the nearby Ashby Canal. Special events are held on Sundays during the summer.

The Cadeby Light Railway, The Old Rectory, Cadeby, Nuneaton, Warwickshire CV13 0AS. Telephone: 0455 290462.

This is the smallest passenger-carrying narrow-gauge railway in England, running along less than 200 yards (180 metres) of track. In addition to the railway there are full-sized traction engines and steam rollers, an extensive model of part of the Great Western Railway and a brass-rubbing centre with over seventy facsimiles.

Great Central Railway, Great Central Station, Great Central Road, Loughborough LE11 1RW. Telephone: 0509 230726.

The Great Central Railway was the last major railway company to open a line in Leicestershire, in 1899. The section south of Leicester is now dismantled and the M1 motorway has been built over the old track. Part of the northern section has been preserved, however, and the 5 mile (8 km) stretch

Rutland Railway Museum: the 0-4-0 saddle-tank locomotive 'Singapore', built in 1936 for Singapore docks. It was captured by the Japanese in the Second World War and is now an honorary member of the Far Eastern Prisoners of War Association.

from Loughborough Central to Rothley is operational, with all trains stopping at Quorn and Woodhouse station. The track is being relaid further south and will continue into Birstall. There are eighteen steam locomotives on the railway, including the only surviving Great Central Railway passenger steam locomotive, number 506 *Butler Henderson*, and the *Duke of Gloucester*. In addition there are also ten diesel engines and a wide variety of rolling stock. The journey takes twenty minutes each way and runs through pleasant countryside; the viaduct across Swithland Reservoir gives particularly charming views of Buddon Wood. All three stations have been restored; the museum and engine sheds are at Loughborough.

Rutland Railway Museum, Cottesmore Iron Ore Mines Siding, Ashwell Road, Cottesmore, Oakham, Rutland LE15 7BX. Telephone: 0572 813203.

Just north of Ashwell, the Cottesmore mineral branch railway, built by the Midland Railway in 1883 to serve local quarries, diverges from the Melton Mowbray to Oakham line. On this branch the Rutland Railway Museum acts as a reminder that much of the railways' traffic was in the movement of minerals: in this area it was iron ore. The

museum is a working steam centre with thirty steam and diesel locomotives, seventy wagons, vans and coaches from nationwide quarries, mines and factories, perhaps the largest collection of freight stock in the United Kingdom.

Tropical Bird Garden, Lindridge Lane, Desford, Leicester LE9 9GN. Telephone: 04557 4603.

There are over fifty different species of birds at the Tropical Bird Garden, including parrots, macaws, cockatoos, toucans and even emus. A particular feature is the use of walk-through aviaries, where a variety of species live harmoniously together.

Twycross Zoo, Twycross, Atherstone, Warwickshire CV9 3PX. Telephone: 0827 880250.

Twycross Zoo was founded in 1963 and is particularly famous for its chimpanzees, although it has a variety of apes and monkeys, such as gorillas, orang-utans and gibbons. There are all sorts of mammals — giraffes, elephants, lions and cheetahs; many species of birds, for example emus, flamingos, parrots and penguins; and a reptile house and Enchanted Forest. Other attractions include a miniature railway and a children's adventure playground.

9
Famous people

Robert Bakewell (1725-95)

Just north-west of Loughborough is the hamlet of Dishley, where Robert Bakewell was born and spent most of his life. Whilst his father farmed at Dishley Grange, Robert was able to travel extensively in England and on the continent of Europe, studying farming methods. After his father's death in 1760 he was able to put his ideas fully into practice. He was concerned to improve the breeding stock of sheep and cattle to provide more meat and was so successful that he hired out one of his rams and received 1200 guineas in fees in one year alone. He also bred horses and was invited to St James's Palace to show one to George III. He was always ready to show people around his farm and discuss his methods, and it may have been his excessive hospitality that caused his bankruptcy in 1776. Despite this setback he continued to farm and died unmarried at the age of seventy.

Frederick Burnaby (1842-85)

Although born in Bedford, where his father was a clergyman, Frederick Burnaby spent much of his time as a child at Somerby. This was because the Reverend Gustavus Burnaby was also Lord of the Manor of that village and patron of the living. A row of cottages at the end of the High Street bears the initials FGB and was a gift to Frederick from his father. In later life he lived at Somerby Hall. He grew up to be an excellent sportsman and frequently hunted with the Quorn. At the age of seventeen he joined the Household Cavalry, rising to the rank of colonel, and served with the regiment until his death at the battle of Abou Klea. He managed nonetheless to take long periods of leave to travel and became a household name when an account of his journey across the steppes of Russia was published in 1876 with the title *A Ride to Khiva*. This sold many thousands of copies and prompted him to write a sequel the following year, *On Horseback through Asia*, which proved almost as popular. At the time of his death he was on his way to relieve General Gordon at Khartoum, and all Britain mourned the death of two national heroes. His widow dedicated the David and Jonathan window in Somerby church to his memory.

James Brudenell, seventh Earl of Cardigan (1797-1868)

The Brudenells of Deene, Northamptonshire, have held the manors of Cranoe and Glooston for several centuries, but the most famous — or infamous — member of the family had further connections with the county. He spent much of his time hunting, before his father bought him a commission in the 8th Hussars. After much scandal both in his public and private life, he became Lieutenant-Colonel of the 11th Light Dragoons. He spent each winter at Brudenell House in Melton

Robert Bakewell,
by John Boultbee.

41

Mowbray for the hunting season, and after the Charge of the Light Brigade retired to Brooksby Hall. He died after a fall from his horse, and his second wife, formerly his mistress, survived him by a number of years. She scandalised the people of Melton by the use of heavy make-up and was reputed to have become so eccentric as to have a coffin made long before her death in 1915, and to have it standing upright in the entrance hall of her house!

Thomas Cook (1808-92)

Thomas Cook was born in Melbourne, Derbyshire, to poor parents and moved to Loughborough in his teens to work for J. F. Winks, a Baptist minister and printer. He spent two years in Rutland as a Bible Reader and Village Missionary for the Baptist church and then in 1830 settled in Market Harborough, where he married Marianne Mason of Barrowden. He became a total abstainer in 1836, and his zeal for the cause of temperance led him to organise a railway excursion from Leicester to Loughborough to attend a meeting on 5th July 1841. No less than 570 people went on the outing at a cost of one shilling each. Thomas Cook moved to Leicester in the same year to found his printing business, which he continued until 1854, by which time his tours had become so successful that he no longer had time for it. The Great Exhibition in 1851 had contributed significantly to the growth of the firm — something like 165,000 visitors went on a Cook's Tour to London to

It is ironic that Thomas Cook should have a pub named in his honour, since he was a strict teetotaller.

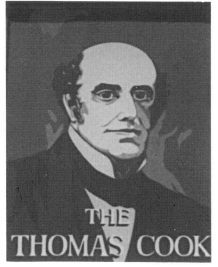

see it in a space of six months. The Paris Exhibition of 1855 led him to start tours to the continent, and his first world tour was organised in 1872. The firm moved its headquarters to London in 1865 and Thomas's son John joined him in partnership. Thomas lived long enough to see the fiftieth anniversary of his travel business, by which time it had grown from one man's hobby to an internationally respected firm with over 1700 employees.

George Fox (1624-91)

The main claim to fame of Fenny Drayton is as the birthplace of the founder of the Society of Friends, the Quakers. It was at the age of nineteen that Fox felt called to leave a settled existence and lead an itinerant life in search of religious truth. He held his first outdoor meeting at Broughton Astley in 1647, but his preaching did not always find favour. He was stoned by a crowd at Market Bosworth in 1649 and imprisoned in the same year for creating a disturbance in St Mary's church, Nottingham. These were to be frequent experiences throughout his life as he travelled to Scotland, Ireland, North America, the West Indies, Germany and Holland. He believed in an individual relationship with God through the Holy Spirit and preached against warfare, capital punishment, the established church and all forms of religious observances. It was left to his disciple Robert Barclay to formalise the beliefs of the Quaker movement.

Lady Jane Grey (1537-54)

It is not known whether Jane was born at Bradgate House or at Groby Old Hall nearby, but it is certain that she spent much of her brief life at Bradgate. It was her misfortune to be fifth in line to the throne after the death of Henry VIII, who was her great-uncle. When Edward VI was crowned, Mary, Elizabeth, Mary Stuart (later Queen of Scots) and Jane's mother, Frances, still took precedence over her. The Duke of Northumberland became Protector late in Edward's reign and arranged that Jane, much against her wishes, should marry his son, that Jane's mother should relinquish her claim to the throne and that the dying Edward VI should name Jane as his heir. The marriage took place on 25th May 1553, and Edward died on 6th July. She was crowned Queen on 10th July but found no support and was deserted by both her father and father-in-law, when in a matter of days Mary took over. Her father was heavily fined and the Duke of Northumberland was beheaded. Jane and her husband were sent to the Tower. They might have been reprieved had Jane's father not become involved in a rebellion against Mary's marriage to Philip of Spain. He and one of his brothers were executed and it was decided that Jane and her husband were too much of a risk and both were beheaded on 12th February 1554. It is said that all the oak trees in Bradgate Park were pollarded as a sign of mourning at her death.

Jeffery Hudson (1619-82)

Born in Oakham probably in 1619, Jeffery Hudson was a dwarf who grew to be 18 inches (46 cm) high by the time he was seven and remained that height until he was thirty, when he grew further, reaching a height of 3 feet 9 inches (114 cm). In an age when midgets were valued as part of any royal or noble household, he was a favourite of George Villiers, Duke of Buckingham, at Burley on the Hill. At a magnificent banquet held there for King Charles I he burst out of a cold pie as the King cut it, much to the amusement of the guests. Queen Henrietta Maria took him back to court and he accompanied her on several journeys to the continent. He seems to have had many adventures, including being captured by pirates, fighting with the Dutch army at Breda and for the Royalist cause in the Civil War. During the Queen's exile in France he fought a duel with a Mr Croft, who had made disparaging remarks about his size, and killed him. He disappeared from court in disgrace and after more adventures found his way back to England in the last years of the Commonwealth. At the Restoration he retired to a quiet life in Rutland but returned to London in 1679, where as a Roman Catholic he was accused of involvement in the Popish Plot and imprisoned for a while. Thereafter he may even have spent some time as a government spy before his death in 1682.

Daniel Lambert (1770-1809)

Although he came of a stout family, Daniel Lambert did not show any signs of unusual weight until he was about 21. At this time he succeeded his father as jailer of the Bridewell prison in Leicester. He appears not to have eaten to excess and was a teetotaller, yet by 1793 he weighed 32 stone (203 kg). He stayed in Leicester until the prison closed in 1805, when he was given a pension by the magistrates of £50 a year in recognition of his services. He then spent part of 1806 in London, where people flocked to see him, even at a charge of one shilling a head. From his home in Leicester he travelled about the country and died in Stamford in 1809. The wall of the Waggon and Horses Inn had to be demolished to remove the corpse and it took more than twenty men to lower his coffin into the grave in St Martin's churchyard. At his death he measured 9 feet 4 inches (2.85 metres) around the waist and weighed 52 stone 11 pounds (335 kg).

Daniel Lambert, by the Leicestershire artist Ben Marshall.

Hugh Latimer (c.1485-1555)

Hugh Latimer was born at Thurcaston, where his father was a yeoman farmer, but the exact date is unknown, as is the site of his birthplace. The house now known as Latimer's House is certainly old enough, but the honour had always been given to another building until it was demolished in 1875. It is not known where he went to school either, but his education continued at Clare College, Cambridge. He was at this time, in his own words, 'as obstinate a Papist as any in England', but gradually changed his views to a more Protestant position. In the uncertain religious climate he found royal favour and was made Bishop of Worcester in 1535, preaching the funeral sermon at Jane Seymour's death in 1537. He was unable to accept the Six Articles of Religion and resigned in 1539. When Henry VIII died in 1547 these were repealed, and for the six-year reign of Edward VI Latimer was able to preach freely. On Mary's accession he was sent to the Tower of London, along with Nicholas Ridley, former Bishop of London, and after refusing to recant the two men were burnt at the stake at Oxford on 16th October 1555. Foxe's *Book of Martyrs* records his final words as 'Be of good comfort Master Ridley, and play the man, we shall this day light such a candle, by God's grace, in England as I trust shall never be put out.'

Joseph Merrick (1862-90)

Only recently has this unfortunate Leicestershire freak regained public attention, due mainly to the success of the film *The Elephant Man*. Merrick was apparently quite normal when born, but neurofibromatosis set in early. This is a formation of tumours in the layers of the skin, which gave the poor man a grossly misshapen appearance and clumsiness. He was thrown out by his father and stepmother at the age of about fifteen and, unable to find work, was finally admitted to the workhouse. To escape, he offered himself as an exhibit in a freak show in 1884. Public opinion was turning against such entertainment in England and the following year he toured in Europe but was deserted and robbed by his manager. He contrived somehow, despite the antagonism and derision that his appalling deformity excited, to return to England and was taken in by Sir Frederick Treves, who cared for him in the last few years of his life.

Titus Oates (1649-1705)

This unsavoury character was born in Oakham and may have acquired some of his worst traits from his father, who at various times was a rabid Anabaptist and a staunch Anglican to suit the current religious feelings of those in power. Titus spent most of his life in trouble. He was expelled from school and failed miserably at university. Somehow he became a clergyman and was vicar of Bobbing, Kent, but in 1673 he was arrested and imprisoned for making false accusations against a Hastings schoolmaster. He escaped and became a naval chaplain but was expelled. He teamed up with a violent anti-Catholic, Dr Israel Tonge, and feigned a conversion to Catholicism to further his designs. He was expelled from Jesuit colleges in Spain and France and on his return to England in 1678 trumped up charges of a 'Popish Plot'. This was readily believed, and a number of people were arrested and executed. The following year suspicion grew about his reliability as a witness, but it was not until 1685 that he was arrested and tried for perjury. He was fined, put in the pillory, publicly whipped and given a life sentence, though he was released four years later. This ignominious life, with its repeated pattern of dishonesty, came to an end in 1705.

John Wyclif (c.1330-84)

The date and town of Wyclif's birth are unknown, though he was probably born in Yorkshire. He studied at Oxford and held several teaching posts at the University, where he mainly resided, although he was Rector of Fillingham, Lincolnshire, and from 1368 to 1384, Rector of Ludgershall in Buckinghamshire. From 1374 he was also Rector of Lutterworth but can have spent little or no time in the parish as his reputation as a scholar increased. He became more and more outspoken in his criticism of the Church, and Pope Gregory XI denounced him in 1377, but royal favour ensured his safety for the time being. His preaching developed a radical political slant and he denied the doctrine of transubstantiation. This led to his losing the protection he had enjoyed, and when in 1382 he was tried for heresy by an ecclesiastical court he was condemned but allowed to retire into obscurity at Lutterworth. It is unlikely that the translation of the Bible that bears his name was entirely his work — much, if not all, was done by his followers John Purvey and Nicholas of Hereford. Wyclif suffered a stroke during mass on 28th December 1384 and died three days later. He was buried in the churchyard, but his body was not allowed to rest in peace, being exhumed in 1428, burnt and the ashes scattered in the river Swift.

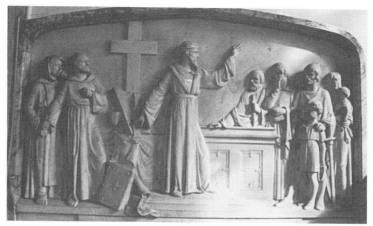

John Wyclif preaching to the people: romanticised relief by Westmacott in Lutterworth church.

10
Hunting, cheese and pork pies

There has always been hunting of some description in Leicestershire and Rutland. In the middle ages foxes were considered vermin and the animals hunted were those that would not only provide good sport but also good meat. Hounds were kept for hunting deer and hare by the nobility and the Abbots of Leicester and Priors of Ulverscroft started a tradition of clerical huntsmen that continues to this day. Little is known about hunting in the county in Tudor and Stuart times, but during this period more and more forest land was turned over to agricultural use and deer became rarer. Foxhunting did not become a notable pastime until the eighteenth century, when Thomas Boothby kept a pack of foxhounds at Tooley Park. In the nineteenth century it became an institution and, although few have the wealth or leisure to indulge in it as in its heyday, it remains an essential part of county life.

The landscape of the county is particularly suited to hunting, especially on the east. It is a tableland and does not get waterlogged, the fields are large and there is still much grassland, with stout hedges. Good horses are needed to stand the pace and the riders must be experienced. Those who hunt with the 'Shire' packs regard other hunts as 'provincials'. One definition of what makes a 'Shire' pack is that it hunts in Leicestershire. This may be too loose a definition for it includes the Atherstone, which is not generally considered a 'Shire' pack, whereas the Pytchley, which hunts only a few parishes in the southern tip of the county, most certainly is. The claims of the Belvoir, Cottesmore, Fernie and Quorn are undisputed.

To appreciate why the hunts have such a hold on the popular imagination it is necessary to relate a little of their history and characters.

about breeding a strain of foxhound best suited to the terrain. He entertained lavishly and many of the nobility were guests at his house parties and followers of his hunt. He was master of the hunt until 1800 but continued to hunt up to his death in 1808. The kennels at Quorn have since been moved to Barrow upon Soar.

At that time the Quorn country included almost the whole of Leicestershire. The northern part of the county was twice loaned to other gentry during the course of the nineteenth century, and the southern part was given in 1852 by the then master, Sir Richard Sutton, to his son and eventually became the Fernie territory. An earlier master was Squire Osbaldeston, a hard-riding man who, after a particularly bad fall was heard to remark, 'I am so unlucky that I think I shall give up hunting', but the sport was so much in his blood that he continued to hunt six days a week until his death, at the age of eighty. In his youth he bet 1000 guineas that he could ride 200 miles (320 km) in ten hours, given unlimited change of horses, and achieved it in under nine. A contemporary of Osbaldeston was the Reverend John Empson, who was such a fine huntsman that he was nicknamed the 'Flying Parson'. It is said that whilst hunting he fell and his horse trod on his nose, which was left hanging by little more than skin. He wrapped his handkerchief around his face to hold it on and set off for the doctor at Oakham, whose skill was such that he was able to stitch it back on, leaving only a slight scar. It is not surprising that the Duke of Wellington remarked at the Battle of Waterloo that the best officers he had on the field were the Leicestershire foxhunters.

The Quorn

Hugo Meynell is rightly considered the founder of modern foxhunting, but the history of the Quorn hounds goes back to Thomas Boothby, of Tooley Park. This mansion has long since been demolished, but Tooley Spinneys, one of the earliest fox covers to be planted, remains, halfway between Earl Shilton and Peckleton. Boothby hunted much of what is now the Quorn country from 1698 until his death in 1752. Meynell came to Quorn the next year and may have taken over some of the hounds. At any rate, he must have been very familiar with the Boothbys, for after the death of his first wife in 1757 he married Thomas Boothby's granddaughter, Anne. Meynell may well have been influenced by Bakewell's systematic breeding of farm animals, for he set

The Belvoir

The history of the Belvoir begins at the same time as that of the Quorn. The Earls of Gainsborough had kept foxhounds since 1695 and in 1728 the fourth Earl joined with the first Earl Gower, the second Viscount Howe, the third Earl of Cardigan and the third Duke of Rutland to form a United Hunt. This lasted only four years, until the death of Lord Cardigan in 1732, and it seems that from then on the Dukes of Rutland kept their own pack at Belvoir. They were masters of the hunt until the end of the nineteenth century, with only one break, from 1830 to 1858, when Lord Forester was in charge. The Belvoir is renowned for the quality of its hounds, both for looks and stamina. The kennels are still at Belvoir.

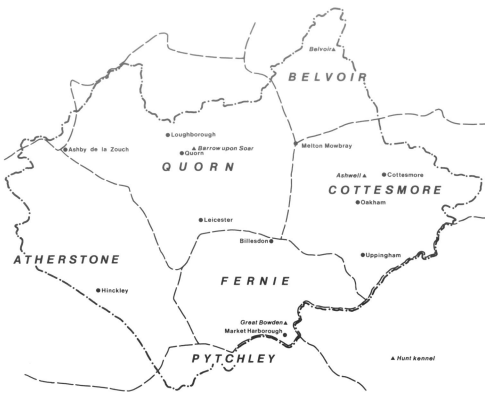

The hunts of Leicestershire and Rutland, showing their territories.

The Cottesmore

Like the Belvoir, the history of the Cottesmore goes back to the Earls of Gainsborough. On the break-up of the United Hunt Lord Gainsborough continued to hunt the Rutland country, and on his death in 1751 his cousin, Tom Noel, inherited his hounds and his widow. In 1788 the hunt passed to Sir William Lowther, later first Earl of Lonsdale, and the hunt was known as the Earl of Lonsdale's for many years until it acquired its new name, the Cottesmore, from the village in which the kennels were situated. They have since been moved to Ashwell.

The Fernie

The elder son of Sir Richard Sutton made such a nuisance of himself on the hunting field that his father exclaimed in anger 'I wish to God you would take 25 couple and break your neck in the damned Harborough country!'

Richard Sutton the younger took him at his word and built kennels at Billesdon, hunting the country for four seasons. William Tailby of Skeffington then collected a pack, kept at Billesdon, and was master of the Billesdon Hunt until 1878, when Sir Bache Cunard took it over. There was at this time an acrimonious dispute about ownership of the territory, since the Quorn claimed it had only been loaned and they wished to reclaim it. The claim was submitted to the hunting committee of Boodle's Club, which resolved the matter by declaring that the country belonged to the Quorn but that the Billesdon should hunt it! The hunt got its name from its next master. Charles Fernie was a young man of delicate health who, in 1888, was advised by his doctors that if he wintered abroad he might survive for five years. Instead, he hunted for 33 years and his wife carried on for a further four years as master. He left his hounds to the hunt on condition that the Quorn give up its claim to the country, to which it magnanimously agreed. The kennels are now at Great Bowden.

Local specialities

Leicestershire can be proud of its achievement in providing Britain with three notable delicacies of more than local fame — Red Leicester and Stilton cheese, and pork pies.

Red Leicester

This cheese was made throughout the county in a large millstone shape, weighing about 45 pounds (20 kg), and acquired a national reputation in the eighteenth century. Its deep colour was produced by using a dye made from carrots, added in the early stages of the cheese-making process. The cheese would be pressed several times during manufacture, usually in a heavy press made from Swithland slate. Thereafter it would be bandaged to form a rind and left to mature for a couple of months. Nowadays it is usually sold in vacuum-packed blocks, but it is well worth asking for mature 'Farmhouse Leicester' in the local cheese shops and markets.

Stilton

Why should this famous Leicestershire cheese bear the name of a village in Cambridgeshire? It is said that in about 1730 a Mrs Paulet of Wymondham was the first to make this cream cheese. She supplied it to the landlord of the Bell Inn, Stilton, on that major coaching route the Great North Road. From there its popularity spread rapidly and dairies throughout Leicestershire exploited the ready market. However, Mrs Paulet's claim to fame is disputed. The historian Nichols records that Mrs Orton of Little Dalby made Stilton cheese in about 1720, but even before then it was known as Quenby cheese or Lady Beaumont's cheese.

The immature cheese is sold as White Stilton, which is milder and more crumbly than Blue Stilton. The latter matures for three months after manufacture, having been pricked to allow oxygen through the rind, which activates the penicillin mould, forming the characteristic blue veins. The pouring of port into a Stilton is frowned on in the best circles, and the practice of scooping cheese from the centre is considered wasteful. The name of Stilton is protected by a trade mark and only cheese made in north-east Leicestershire and just over the border in Nottinghamshire and one solitary outpost in Derbyshire, may be given that noble title.

Pork pies

Melton Mowbray pork pies have not been renowned for as long as Stilton cheese but nonetheless have a history going back as far as 1831, when Edward Adcock made them commercially for the first time. There is, however, a link between the two because the whey, which is a by-product of cheese-making, was fed as a very effective fattener to the pigs. Stilton owes its fame to a coaching inn: Melton pies owe theirs to hunting. A portion of pork pie was easily carried as sustenance during a long day's hunting, and the influx of nobility with all their retainers each winter, not only from all parts of England but from Europe as well, ensured that the fame of Melton pies spread far and wide.

The pastry case is raised by hand around a block, not made in a tin, so bowed sides are a sign of the genuine article. It is filled with finely chopped pork, seasoned and moulded into a ball fitting just inside the case, and finally a jelly made from the bones is poured in after the pie has been baked. Traditionally made pork pies are still sold in Melton Mowbray but the days when this was the major industry in the town are long past.

The Boxing Day meet of the Quorn Hunt at Loughborough.

The Old Grammar School at Appleby Parva.

11
Towns and villages

APPLEBY MAGNA

Appleby is close to the borders with Derbyshire, Staffordshire and Warwickshire, and has several attractive houses of the sixteenth, seventeenth and eighteenth centuries and three other buildings of particular note. The church, St Michael, is fourteenth-century, with some of its original stained glass, but the interior mainly dates from the restoration of 1830 — box pews, west gallery and plaster vaulting. Of the medieval moated manor house only the fifteenth-century stone gate-house survives, with a timber-framed house built alongside in the following century. This may be seen from the footpath behind the Post Office in Mawbys Lane. In nearby Appleby Parva stands the Old Grammar School, founded by Sir John Moore at the end of the seventeenth century. This is a fine three-storey building with two wings, an arcade on the ground floor and a cupola on the roof. It is now the village primary school — surely one of the grandest in England.

ASHBY DE LA ZOUCH

Early closing Wednesday; market day Saturday.

Ashby de la Zouch is a pleasant country town. Henry III granted a charter in 1219 permitting a weekly market and four annual fairs. This accounts for the width of Market Street, where the regular market is still held. Some of the buildings in this road are timber-framed, dating from the sixteenth century, though most have later facades and others are Georgian. None is architecturally outstanding but all jostle together without any seeming out of place. There are no longer four fairs, but the annual September Statutes Fair is one of the highlights of the town's calendar. It was in former years the venue for the annual hiring of farm servants but is now largely a funfair. Ashby's prosperity was at its height in the early nineteenth century, when water was pumped from the saline springs at Moira to make it a spa town. The Ivanhoe Baths, so called because Sir Walter Scott in *Ivanhoe* describes a tournament at the castle of Ashby de la Zouch in which his hero defeated the Black Knight, were built in 1822, two years after the novel's publication. They were demolished in 1962, but the Royal Hotel of 1826 and nearby Rawdon Terrace still testify to the town's former glory. The monument opposite, rather like one of the Eleanor crosses, was erected in 1879 in memory of the Countess of Loudon.

The castle (see chapter 5) and the church, St Helen, lie away from the main route through the town. The church was probably built in the mid to late fifteenth century, about the same time as the castle. It was extended by the addition of outer aisles during the restoration of 1878-80, and the alabaster font and pulpit were installed at this time. There is a variety of stained glass roundels from the fourteenth to sixteenth centuries in the windows of the chancel and the Hastings Chapel. Also in the chapel are monuments to the Earls of Huntingdon. Francis, the second Earl, who died in 1561, is depicted with his wife on a table tomb. Theophilus, the ninth Earl, who died in 1746, is commemorated not by a sculpture of himself but by one of his mourning widow, Selina. She was a notable supporter of the Wesleys and of George Whitefield and founded the chapels known as the Countess of Huntingdon's Connexion. Several hatchments hang in this chapel. In the north aisle is the fifteenth century effigy of a pilgrim, probably one of the Hastings family, and in the south aisle a painted wooden bust of Margery Wright (died 1623). Notice the finger pillory at the west end of the church, used to display offenders to public view.

BILLESDON
The main A47 Leicester to Uppingham road now bypasses Billesdon and the village is much quieter as a result. It is, however, the largest village on this route and a weekly market was held here in earlier centuries. The most interesting buildings are grouped around the church of St John Baptist, which is largely thirteenth-century but much restored in the 1860s. The Old School, built of ironstone in 1650, lies just to the east and the Vicarage, also built in stone in the seventeenth century, with brick additions of the two following centuries, is just to the south. The Vicarage wall is made of a stone base and the upper part of mud or cob. So too is the barn opposite the Old School.

The bypass also enables the ridge and furrow of the medieval system of strip farming to the north of the village to be clearly seen, and the motorist gets an uninterrupted view of Billesdon Coplow, the prominent clump of trees to the north-west. From this covert began the most famous run in the annals of the Quorn Hunt on 24th February 1800. Hounds ran from here in a semicircle to Aylestone before changing fox and carrying on to Enderby Gorse, a distance of 28 miles (45 km) covered in two and a quarter hours. Only four riders managed to keep up with them right to the finish!

BUCKMINSTER
Nothing is left now of the Anglo-Saxon monastery that is indicated by the 'minster' element in the name of this village. No part of the present church, St John Baptist, is earlier than the thirteenth century, and much dates from the following century. Its most unusual feature is the octagonal stone staircase in the south-east corner of the nave that leads to the tower and rood loft. Buckminster is a well kept estate village with a large green and mainly Victorian cottages, though the manor it served, Buckminster Hall, was demolished in 1952.

CASTLE DONINGTON
Early closing Wednesday.
The castle from which Castle Donington takes its name is now merely a mound on the northern edge of the village. It was built to command the crossing points of the river Trent in the eleventh or twelfth century, demolished in 1216 and rebuilt later that century. It passed to the Hastings family in 1461 but fell into decay, as they lived mostly at Ashby de la Zouch, and was finally demolished in 1595. Francis Rawdon Hastings, second Earl of Moira, built Donington Hall west of the village in 1790. The grounds are now used as a motor-racing circuit and the Donington Collection (see chapter 6) is housed here. With the East Midlands Airport (see chapter 6) just south of the village, Castle Donington is less peaceful than it once was.

The church bears the unusual dedication to St Edward, King and Martyr, and its fine spire is a landmark for miles around. It is recorded in the Domesday Book, but the church as it now stands is mainly thirteenth- and fourteenth-century. Leicestershire has only 25 surviving monumental brasses and one of the better ones is here: Robert de Staunton, depicted in armour with his wife, who died in 1458, under an elaborate canopy. Another tomb-chest has the alabaster effigies of Robert Hazylrygg (died 1529) and his wife.

There are some interesting houses in the village. Key House in the High Street is timber-framed and dates from 1636. Do not be misled by the datestone on the two-storey porch: although it is dated 1595, it originally came from another building. Lower down the hill are good seventeenth- and eighteenth-century houses, an early nineteenth-century Gothick cottage and several sixteenth-century cruck-built cottages. In the street curiously named Baroon is the Friends' Meeting House of 1829.

CHURCH LANGTON
Church Langton is the central village of the five settlements collectively called 'The Langtons'. West Langton comprises Langton Hall and East Langton is little more than an estate village. **Thorpe Langton** is about the same size but has a church, St Leonard, built around 1300 but poorly restored in 1868. **Tur Langton** church was also in a bad state of repair in the 1860s and was demolished. A new church,

dedicated to St Andrew, was erected on a site further east in 1865. It is a brash red-brick building, a delight to those who enjoy Victorian architecture but a little out of place deep in the countryside.

Church Langton was the original settlement of the five and the mother church of the group. Its church, St Peter, is a noble building with a high tower that dominates the surrounding countryside. It dates from the late thirteenth and early fourteenth centuries, replacing an earlier Norman church. Most of the old fittings were removed during the restoration of 1865-6, but some monuments and the font of 1662 remain. The organ has been rebuilt, but its case is still the original of 1759 which was installed by William Hanbury for the first of his music festivals, held that year. Hanbury was rector of the parish and his two ruling passions were music and botany. He hoped that the profits from his nurseries and concerts would fund his scheme for a huge collegiate church and seat of learning at Church Langton but, although his charitable foundation did much good work in the neighbourhood, this never materialised. Shortly after his death in 1778 his son built instead a very fine red-brick rectory for himself. Earlier rectors include Polydore Vergil, who wrote a 26-volume history of England published in 1533, and Laurence Saunders, who was burnt at the stake during the reign of Queen Mary.

COALVILLE

This place-name gives a remarkably accurate picture of the town. 'Coal' denotes the principal industry of the town and 'ville' is an attempt to lend tone to the area by using the French word for 'town'. The settlement was originally known as Long Lane and grew rapidly in size when Whitwick Colliery opened in 1822, quickly followed by Snibston Colliery in 1833. In the same year the Leicester to Swannington railway reached the town. There was never any overall plan for development so, other than the clock tower, which is a war memorial, there are no public or private buildings of note in this urban sprawl.

HALLATON

In medieval times Hallaton was one of the more important villages in the south-east of the county, with a weekly market and four fairs a year. There was a motte and bailey castle here in the twelfth century (see chapter 3) protecting the iron workings, and the church of St Michael and All Angels is substantial, as befits a prosperous community. Evidence of an earlier settlement is the Saxon grave cover in the north-west corner of the church. Norman work survives in the capitals of the north aisle, and notably in the tympanum, now set in the north porch, which depicts the Archangel thrusting his spear through the dragon's head. Much work was done on the church in the thirteenth century — the tower and spire are good examples of this period — and the aisles were widened and given windows with flowing tracery in the next century. Most of the stained glass is by Kempe, and was installed in the 1880s and 1890s.

The village has a duck pond at the north end

Hallaton Bottle Kicking. The three bottles are held aloft, preceded in the procession by the hare pie.

and a small village green at the south with a conical butter cross that looks more like a lock-up. Between is an interesting variety of seventeenth- and eighteenth-century houses and cottages, some of them thatched. To the south of the village lies Hare Pie Bank, which is the starting place of the annual Easter Monday Bottle-Kicking. Opposing teams from Hallaton and the neighbouring village of Medbourne gather at the Fox and Goose, by the duck pond, and process to Hare Pie Bank holding aloft the bottle, which is in fact a small keg. Hare pie is 'distributed' to the crowd by being tossed over them from a sack, and the Bottle-Kicking begins. The bottle is thrown in the air and each team tries by whatever means to get it to the other side of the stream at the bottom of the hill. This inevitably results in a muddy scrummage, making it difficult for spectators to follow; nonetheless this is a very popular event.

HINCKLEY
Early closing Thursday; market days Monday and Saturday.

It is the proud boast of Hinckley that the first stocking frame in the county was set up here in 1640. Hosiery became the principal industry in the town and still employs people here. In Lower Bond Street is a row of thatched timber-framed cottages built in the seventeenth century with additional windows to give more light for the frame-workers. Atkins' late nineteenth-century hosiery factory stands behind them. Nearby is the Great Meeting (Unitarian chapel) of 1722, looking very much like a private house. Little of old Hinckley survives. There are the castle mound and the parish church, dedicated to the Assumption of St Mary and built in the fourteenth century. The tower is of this date but the spire was rebuilt in 1788. The church was over-restored in the 1860s and 1870s. Hinckley is one of the few places in the county mentioned by Shakespeare. Its fair was sufficiently famous to be referred to in *Henry IV, Part II*.

HORNINGHOLD
Leicestershire has few 'picture postcard' villages, but this is one, largely because of the Hardcastle family of Blaston Hall, who restored the original cottages and built new ones in a similar style at the end of the nineteenth century and the beginning of the twentieth, taking great care over the layout of the village. The church, St Peter, was not restored and retains many interesting features. The earliest is the Norman doorway with three tiers of a star design around the arch which has been reset in the south aisle. Like much of the rest of the building this dates from the thirteenth century. There are several medieval bench ends and an eighteenth-century communion

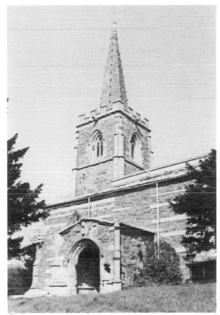

Hungarton church.

rail. The rest of the fittings were installed in 1844, uninfluenced by the fashion for Gothic that was just beginning to sweep England.

HUNGARTON
It is fortunate that Hungarton is not a busy village as its main street is a series of right-angled bends. The man responsible for this was Shukbrugh Ashby, who rebuilt much of the village in the third quarter of the eighteenth century, giving it a pleasant unity of design. His monument may be seen in the church, St John Baptist, along with those of his forebears. The church is built of limestone and ironstone, now somewhat decaying. The tower, like the rest of the building, is fourteenth-century and, in common with many local churches, has several grotesque gargoyles. Inside, the oldest feature is the Norman font. The Quenby Chapel takes up half the south aisle and is enclosed by a fifteenth-century parclose screen. There are six hatchments and an early Victorian organ in a Gothic case made by Forster and Andrews of Hull in 1849.

Within the parish are three country houses, Baggrave, Ingarsby Old Hall and Quenby, their nearby villages all depopulated in the late fifteenth century. Baggrave is set in parkland and can be seen from the unfenced road that runs past it. It was built in the sixteenth century, though little of this is apparent since the rebuilding of about 1750 has given it a typical Georgian look. The east wing of Ingarsby Old Hall may date from the late fifteenth century but could be of about 1540, after the dissolution of Leicester Abbey, which formerly owned the property. The remainder dates from the seventeenth century. Quenby Hall is approached along a fine avenue of trees, which serves as a public bridleway between Hungarton and Cold Newton. The house is a splendid example of early seventeenth-century architecture, somewhat conservative in style, based on a central range with two wings in an H plan. It is three storeys high, of red brick with a diamond pattern of blue bricks and stone dressings. Not content with rebuilding Hungarton, Shukbrugh Ashby rebuilt Quenby Hall as well, but his alterations were reversed early in the twentieth century to restore the original style. The house and grounds are occasionally open to the public.

HUSBANDS BOSWORTH

Travelling through on the main east-west or north-south roads, the casual visitor misses most of the interest of this village. In Honeypot Lane is a brick and timber-framed house of 1712 and elsewhere there are later brick-built houses. The Baptist Chapel of 1807 is also brick. It is unusual to find a stone-built Roman Catholic church in a village, but one was founded here in 1873 by Sir Francis Turville, who lived in the Hall. Fortunately its lavish interior has survived the liturgical reforms of the Roman Catholic church. The parish church, All Saints, has a fourteenth-century tower with a spire rebuilt after being struck by lightning in 1755. The rest of the church has been much restored.

IBSTOCK

This is a large village in the west Leicestershire coalfield and mining has played a marked part in its development, though it is perhaps better known for its brickworks. There is little of note other than the church, which is mainly fourteenth-century. William Laud, later to become Archbishop of Canterbury, was Rector of Ibstock from 1614 to 1626.

KEGWORTH

Early closing Wednesday.

Always a sizable village, Kegworth formerly had a weekly market and regular fairs. It lies just west of the river Soar and was in a good position to profit from the increased trade along the river when it was improved to take canal traffic. The main industry in the nineteenth century was framework knitting, and a workshop with windows running the length of the building may still be seen behind the Britannia Inn. There are some good houses and cottages, in particular a timber-framed house near the church and a large

brick-built house of 1698 with a roof of Swithland slate. The church, St Andrew, has a fine tower and spire, built like the rest of the church in the late thirteenth and early fourteenth century. The royal arms, dating from 1684, are prominently displayed, as originally decreed, above the chancel arch. An earlier wooden coat of arms of about 1500 is now above the vestry door.

KETTON

The quarries of Ketton have provided limestone for many churches and cathedrals in England, which makes it all the more curious that the church, St Mary, is built of Barnack stone. Building started in the late twelfth century and the tower and west front date from this period. The aisles were added between 1230 and 1240 and the beautiful broach spire seems to have taken about fifty years to complete. Ketton stone was used for headstones in the churchyard, and one near the lychgate is to a stone-mason, William Hibbins, who died in 1785. The tools of his trade are engraved on his tombstone. His descendants built a house on Stocks Hill with an amazing wealth of architectural detail in a wide variety of styles. Most of the houses in the village are of the same butter-coloured stone and all are attractive. On the road towards Stamford is the Ketton cement works — one of the largest employers in the area. Fortunately it does not detract too much from the rest of the village.

LANGHAM

Langham, large by Rutland standards, also has a major employer — Ruddle's Brewery. The church of St Peter and St Paul has much Perpendicular detail, especially the south transept with its delicate window tracery and the fine slender spire. The clerestory is unusual in that there are windows to the east as well as to the north and south. The church was originally a chapelry of Oakham and has much in common with its mother-church, though the interior is less interesting. There are still some good stone houses in the village, mainly around the church.

LAUNDE

The appeal of Launde lies as much in its setting as in its history or architecture. The house is surrounded by parkland and woods in a hollow of the rolling hills of east Leicestershire. An Augustinian priory was founded here in 1119. This suffered the same fate as other monasteries in 1538, but the last prior had been astute enough to dispose of most of its assets before Thomas Cromwell, Henry VIII's right-hand man, claimed Launde for himself. The chancel of the priory church survives as the private chapel of the house.

Some fifteenth-century stained glass can be seen and also the tomb of Gregory Cromwell, Thomas's son, who died in 1551. It is unusual for such a large monument not to have an effigy of the deceased, only his coat of arms. The house is mainly seventeenth-century with nineteenth-century alterations. It has now returned to a spiritual use as the Retreat House for the Diocese of Leicester. The warden is willing to show visitors the chapel on request. Just north of the house are monastic fishponds and an eighteenth-century ice house.

LEICESTER
Early closing Thursday; principal market days Wednesday, Friday and Saturday.

The city of Leicester is the hub of the county and is centrally situated so that few places are more than a half-hour drive away. Its 1981 population was about 280,000, and it is not in itself a notable tourist attraction. However, the following walk takes in most of the more interesting places, slight detours being marked in brackets. Other places are mentioned at the end of this itinerary or in the preceding chapters.

All directions in Leicester seem to start 'You know the Clock Tower....', so that is probably the best point to begin. The **Clock Tower** was built in 1868 to a design by the local architect Joseph Goddard, and at each corner is a statue. One is of Simon de Montfort and the others are of benefactors to the city: William Wyggeston, Sir Thomas White and Alderman Newton. Walk south along Gallowtree Gate, one of the main shopping centres, and notice immediately on your right the **Thomas Cook Building,** with terracotta panels between the first and second floors depicting the first excursion to Loughborough in 1841. Cross the junction with Halford and Horsefair Streets and go along Granby Street. On the left is the **Turkey Cafe,** an oriental design with Doulton tiles and a turkey cock at the top of the facade. On the corner of Granby Street and Bishop Street is the **Midland Bank,** built in 1872 of red brick with curious stone beasts at the angles and some excellent stained glass. Turn right into Bishop Street. Across Town Hall Square may be seen the **Town Hall** itself, built in Queen Anne style in 1873-6 by an otherwise obscure Leicester architect, F. J. Hames, who in 1879 also designed the splendid fountain with its winged lions.

Continue along Bishop Street, with the **Methodist Church** of 1815 on the left, and turn left in Bowling Green Street. Turn right in Belvoir Street and on the opposite side of the road is the **City Library,** a not unattractive Regency building. Belvoir Street becomes Welford Place.

(On the left is Wellington Street, which

The focal point of Leicester: the Clock Tower.

may be felt worth a brief detour to see some of the nineteenth century industrial buildings and **Holy Cross Priory,** home of the Dominicans. The first church, built in 1817, is now a parish centre, and the main church was started in 1928 but not finished until 1958. Also branching off Welford Place is King Street, again worth a detour. At the far end is some of the best early nineteenth-century architecture in the city, **The Crescent,** a concave terrace of three-storey brick houses, and **Crescent Cottages,** a charming group of two-storey stuccoed villas. **Holy Trinity church** opposite, on Regent Road, was originally of 1838 but remodelled in 1871-2 by S. S. Teulon in a bold, almost quirky Gothic style with an over-ornate tower and spire. The interior has been refurbished beyond recognition. Leading off King Street is **New Walk,** a promenade laid out in 1785, which climbs gently out of the centre as far as Victoria Park. It passes Holy Cross Priory and the **Museum and Art Gallery** [see chapter 6], and although there are some modern intrusions, most of the building is pleasant nineteenth-century work.)

Back in Welford Place is the facade of the **Phoenix Assurance Offices;** the rest of the building was demolished in 1974. On the corner of Welford Place and Welford Road is the **New Walk Centre**, the modern City Council offices. Turn left into Welford Road, then right into York Road, then right again into Oxford Street. The former **Congregational chapel**, built in 1862, is now quite transformed with an exciting facade of white marble imported from India. It is the European headquarters of the Jain faith, and the sculptures represent elements of that belief. Immediately opposite is the **Clephan Building** of the Polytechnic, originally a hosiery works, with Gothic and Art Nouveau motifs. The Polytechnic campus is fairly compact with a variety of buildings, some purpose-built, such as the tower block, and others taken over from industrial use.

Marooned in the centre of the road is the **Magazine** (see chapter 6), which can be reached only by using the subway. This is also the best way to get to the **Newarke** and the **Newarke Houses Museum** (see chapter 6). Turn right past the museum into Castle View. This is one of the most picturesque parts of Leicester, looking along the cobbled street to the **Turret Gateway**, built in 1422 and ruined in election rioting in 1832, and beyond to the spire of **St Mary de Castro**. Behind the eighteenth-century houses on the left is the original **Castle Mound**, which is perhaps better

Leicester Cathedral from the west.

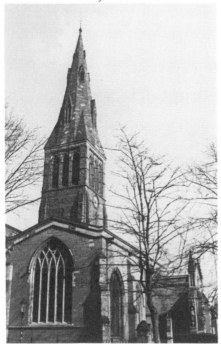

seen from the Castle Gardens. In Castle Yard is the **Court House**, with a brick front of about 1695. Behind it, however, is the Norman Great Hall, now divided into courts but nonetheless a very solid building. The timber-framed **Gatehouse** of 1446, leading to Castle Street, is just as picturesque as the Turret Gateway in its own fashion.

The first major church on this itinerary is **St Mary de Castro**. It would seem to have been founded around 1107 as a collegiate chapel, and the arcading inside the nave on the south and west walls may date from this time. Building went on throughout the Norman period and the finest feature is the triple sedilia in the chancel. Another can be found in the thirteenth-century south aisle. This aisle is such a major addition to the church that it would seem to have been built specifically for the use of the parish. The tower was crammed into the west end of this aisle for lack of space. The exceptionally elegant spire was probably erected in the following century. The church was thoroughly restored during the nineteenth century and most of the fittings are from that date. The font is thirteenth-century, however, and there are some good fourteenth-century heraldic tiles.

From Castle Street, use the footbridge to cross St Nicholas Circle, as this gives a good view of the **Jewry Wall** (see chapter 3). Vaughan College and the **Jewry Wall Museum** (see chapter 6) are on the left. **St Nicholas church** is the only one in the city with any Saxon fabric left. The walls of the nave are from the late Saxon period, evidenced by the two small windows with reused Roman tiles in the north wall. The base of the tower is Norman, as are the chancel and the south door. The south aisle is thirteenth-century and retains its original sedilia and piscina. The font is finely carved fourteenth-century work with a good modern cover.

Dodging the traffic on St Nicholas Circle, cross to St Nicholas Place. Left, along Highcross Street, can be seen the **Grammar School** of 1573, poorly restored.

(Leaving the itinerary, the High Street has many interesting commercial details above street level, such as the large frying pan above Griffins hardware store, the tiles of the old Singer Sewing Machine Company and of Hamptons the Chemist, and the chubby nudes of the Electric Theatre, the earliest surviving cinema building in the city.)

Returning to St Nicholas Place, swing right until it becomes pedestrianised at Applegate. Here are **Wygston's House Museum of Costume** (see chapter 6) and, opposite, **Alderman Newton's School**, now the Leicester Grammar School. Turn left into Guidhall Lane and on the right is the **Guildhall** (see chapter 6). Between the Guildhall and the Cathedral turn

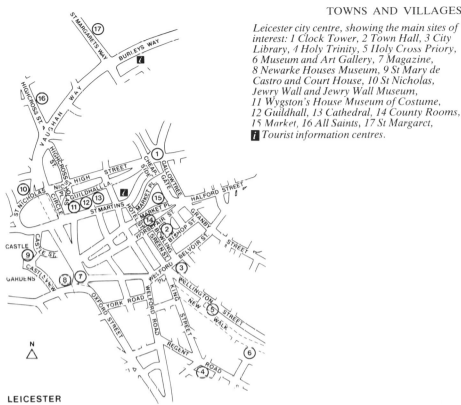

Leicester city centre, showing the main sites of interest: 1 Clock Tower, 2 Town Hall, 3 City Library, 4 Holy Trinity, 5 Holy Cross Priory, 6 Museum and Art Gallery, 7 Magazine, 8 Newarke Houses Museum, 9 St Mary de Castro and Court House, 10 St Nicholas, Jewry Wall and Jewry Wall Museum, 11 Wygston's House Museum of Costume, 12 Guildhall, 13 Cathedral, 14 County Rooms, 15 Market, 16 All Saints, 17 St Margaret, *i* Tourist information centres.

LEICESTER

right into a narrow passage, St Martins West, which leads into St Martins. The **Cathedral** is best seen from the south, with its imposing tower and broach spire of 1867, modelled on that at Ketton. It has been so thoroughly restored that externally it seems to be almost entirely Victorian, and the appalling landscaping of the churchyard, with a fountain and gravestones standing upright like dominoes waiting to be pushed over, detracts from its dignity. It was originally the parish church of St Martin and always of civic importance, being elevated to cathedral status in 1927. The Saxon bishops probably used St Nicholas as their cathedral, until the city fell to the Danes in the ninth century. The furnishings are mainly twentieth-century, but there are three fifteenth-century stalls in the chancel, a magnificent late seventeenth-century pulpit with sounding board, and the eighteenth-century Archdeacon's Court.

Emerging from the Cathedral, turn left into St Martins, and one cannot fail to see the **National Westminster Bank**, a monumental edifice of Portland stone built in 1900. It is very ambitious, with columns and domes, and designed to impress on the passer-by the

stability and permanence of Parr's Bank, for whom it was erected. Turn right and walk along Hotel Street to the elegant **County Rooms**, built at the end of the eighteenth century as a hotel and ballroom. The upper floor has three large windows for the ballroom and two niches with statues of the muses. Turning left into the Market Place, notice on the right the old **Fish Market** of 1881, now gutted, with modern buildings under its canopy. On the wall is part of a fourth-century tessellated pavement. There is always a market in the square, which is roofed over. The **Corn Exchange** still stands; built in the 1850s, its most spectacular element is the bridge-like staircase to the upper floor. Nearby the fifth Duke of Rutland smiles benignly from his pedestal. Leave the Market Place at the north corner and walk through Cheapside, which has become Leicester's Speakers' Corner. The **High Cross**, simply a column surmounted by a ball and cross, came from the dome that once stood at the junction of High Street and Highcross Street. As one emerges into High Street, the Clock Tower will be visible, marking the end of this tour.

There are two more medieval churches in

Leicester. **All Saints** in Highcross Street is Norman, but with much rebuilding carried out in about 1300 and the top of the tower built a century or so later. It is now redundant and rarely open to the public. **St Margaret**, on the corner of Burleys Way and St Margarets Way, is a fine church with a tall tower. A levy to rebuild this tower was ordered by the Bishop of Lincoln in 1444 and, although there is earlier work, much of the outward appearance of the church dates from this time. It is a spendid, spacious building, unfortunately isolated from the city centre by the inner ring road.

To the south of the city centre, between the Welford Road and London Road, is **Victoria Park**. This is much frequented by those who live nearby, though it has no amusement facilities like Abbey Park. Along its north-western edge is the **University**. The main building was originally the Leicestershire Lunatic Asylum, built in 1837, and was opened as a college in 1921, achieving the status of a university in 1957. Much has been built since on what is rather a cramped site. The Attenborough Building of 1968 is the tallest and was named after a principal of the college, F. L. Attenborough, best known nationally as the father of two notable sons, Sir Richard and Sir David. It is the Engineering Building of 1959, however, that is considered the most interesting and striking

The Carillon at Loughborough.

example of modern architecture, not only in the University but in the whole of the county. Next to the University is the **War Memorial,** a massive triumphal arch designed by Sir Edwin Lutyens. The city's major concert hall, the **De Montfort Hall**, is at the northern tip of the park.

LOUGHBOROUGH
Early closing Wednesday; market days Thursday and Saturday.

Loughborough is now the largest town in the county apart from Leicester. It was a substantial village in medieval times and was granted a market and two annual fairs in the reign of Henry III. One of the fairs still takes place each year for three days in early November. Only two buildings are left of medieval Loughborough — the Old Rectory (see chapter 6) and the parish church, All Saints, both dating from the fourteenth century. The most obviously early parts of the church are the north and south arcades. The very fine tower and the clerestory are fifteenth-century, but the rest was thoroughly restored by Sir George Gilbert Scott in 1860. He spared a curious font that may be Elizabethan, an eighteenth-century alabaster altar table with wrought iron supports, and two interesting monuments. One is to Joanna Walters (died 1673), in which both she and two of her children are shown in shrouds, and the other to George Tate (died 1822) by Westmacott. Since the town grew so rapidly, particularly in the nineteenth century, a further five Anglican churches have been built, of which only Emmanuel, built by Rickman in 1835, is of any architectural merit. The large brick Baptist chapel dates from 1828 and St Mary's Roman Catholic church was built in a Greek style in 1833, only four years after the Catholic Emancipation Act.

The earliest secular buildings are grouped around the parish church. Behind the seventeenth-century facades of two houses lie fifteenth-century timber-framed dwellings and there are several pleasant eighteenth-century houses. There is some interesting Victorian architecture in the Market Place, notably the Town Hall and the banks, but the twentieth century predominates. The University of Technology to the west of the town has some adventurous buildings. The Carillon Tower in Queen's Park may seem an unusual choice for a war memorial. Its ground floor houses some relics of two world wars, but it was built primarily for the carillon of 47 bells. Recitals are given regularly in the summer months. It is not perhaps such a surprising choice when the largest bell foundry in England, Taylors, is to be found in the town (see chapter 6). It was the canals — the Soar Navigation, opened in 1778, and the Leicester Navigation of 1794 — that helped the town become such an industrial centre in the nineteenth century. John Heathcoat established his machine-made lace factory here in 1809, but in 1816 his machines were smashed by Luddites and he closed the factory, moving to Tiverton, Devon. Hosiery in general flourished, however, and that and engineering became the principal industries of Loughborough.

LUTTERWORTH
Early closing Wednesday; market day Thursday.

Lutterworth is halfway between Rugby and Leicester and was a convenient coaching stop along the route. It has always been a small country town and seems to have been at its most prosperous in the early nineteenth century, if the buildings in the town centre are an accurate guide. The Denbigh Arms and the Greyhound are both of this period, as is the United Reformed chapel, despite its datestone of 1777. The Town Hall was built in a classical style in 1836, and many of the larger private houses and terraces bear similar stylistic hallmarks. There are earlier buildings, notably a row of timber-framed and thatched cottages in Bell Street, and the church, St Mary. Like so many in the county, this dates from the late thirteenth and early fourteenth centuries. It is a large building, but the most prominent features are the pinnacles on the tower that are disproportionate in size. They were erected after the spire was destroyed by winds in 1703. Inside the church above the chancel arch is a restored wall painting of the Last Judgement; another in the north aisle represents three kings. There are two fifteenth-century brasses and an alabaster monument to an unknown knight and his lady. The pulpit is also fifteenth-century and therefore too late to have been the one from which John Wyclif delivered his sermons (see chapter 9). He is depicted in a marble relief of 1837, preaching to his people. One of his successors, Robert Sutton, is almost forgotten. He died a martyr's death: hanged, drawn and quartered in 1594 for reverting to the Roman Catholic faith.

MARKET BOSWORTH
Market day Wednesday.

This pleasant market town must be the smallest in the county, scarcely larger than many of the nearby villages. A royal charter granted in 1285 gave the right to hold a market and two fairs, and the town acquired the prefix 'Market' to distinguish it from Husbands Bosworth, that is 'Bosworth of the farmers'. Two hundred years later it gave its name to the final battle in the Wars of the Roses and the battlefield is now a tourist attraction (see chapter 8). The same site was also the scene of a skirmish in 1644 during the Civil War. Throughout the middle ages the Harcourt family, whose name survives in two villages in the county, Kibworth Harcourt and Newton Harcourt, held the manor of Bosworth and one of their number, Robert, fought against Richard III. He died childless in 1509 and the estate passed through a succession of owners before being bought in 1589 by the other family most closely associated with Bosworth, the Dixies. While the senior member of this family lived in the hall, another relative, sometimes a younger brother, would be the Rector.

The church, St Peter, is quite large and dates from the early fourteenth century; the tower and spire are particularly fine. The base of the font may be thirteenth-century, but the bowl can be dated to between 1350 and 1360 by the shields carved on each of the six sides. The sedilia, piscina and squint are all fifteenth-century. There is a lavish monument to the Reverend John Dixie, who died in 1719. The weeping figure of a lady, reclining uncomfortably on a pile of books, is his sister Margaret. She may well have written the fulsome Latin inscription. The hall is no longer in private hands but has become the Bosworth Park Infirmary. There are some interesting houses and public buildings in the town. In the Market Place are a pair of cruck-built cottages, with a nineteenth-century facade, which makes them look like rather charming estate cottages with latticed windows and steep gables. There is also a group of seventeenth century half-timbered thatched cottages, but many buildings date from the eighteenth and early nineteenth centuries. Note in particular the Tudor-style Grammar School of 1828 (Samuel Johnson was usher at the Dixie Grammar School in 1731), and the classical Workhouse of 1836.

MARKET HARBOROUGH
Early closing Wednesday; market days Tuesday and Saturday.

Market Harborough is a comparatively late settlement, first mentioned in 1177, that grew up at a crossing of the river Welland. Since it was within the parish of Great Bowden all burials took place there, which is why there has never been a graveyard around the church. Now it has eclipsed all the surrounding villages and is the largest town in the south of the county, with a variety of industry, which fortunately does not detract from the old town centre. It is the church which dominates the scene. Its fourteenth-century limestone tower and spire soar high above all the other buildings and draw the eye. When floodlit at night it is especially impressive. The rest of the church cannot compare with it, though anywhere else the ironstone nave with clerestory, north and south aisles and long chancel would be thought noteworthy. The interior has been

The Three Swans at Market Harborough, the county's most outstanding inn sign.

The Old Grammar School at Market Harborough.

over-restored and it is surprising that the north and south galleries survived. The church has the unusual dedication of St Dionysius.

The High Street, north of the church, was the original market place. Here are the two main coaching inns, the Angel and the Three Swans, with its famous inn sign. Even after the days of the stage coaches the stabling was much in demand, for the town was a good central point for hunting with the Fernie or the Pytchley hounds. There is much good Georgian building, including the Old Town Hall at the angle of Church Street and High Street, which was built by the fourth Lord Harborough in 1788. The other building of note is the classical Congregational chapel of 1844. Just south of the church is the Old Grammar School, founded in 1607, the open ground floor of which served as a market. East of that, in Adam and Eve Street, are the Council Offices, which also house the Library and Museum (see chapter 6). This was originally the Symington corset factory, built in 1889. The southern part of the old town has been spoilt by modern development.

MARKET OVERTON

There was a market held here some time prior to 1200, when the full name of the village was first recorded. It was granted a charter for a market and fair in 1315, but the last mention of any being held was in 1338! There is evidence of Roman occupation between Market Overton and Thistleton. It was apparently quite a substantial settlement, with a temple complex as well as furnaces for smelting ironstone, pottery kilns and a villa nearby. Coins and pottery of the Coritani were found here as well as Roman, which suggests that it was a market centre even before the Roman period. The Saxons too left their mark and two Anglo-Saxon cemeteries have been excavated. The tower arch inside the church is of this period. The rest of the church of St Peter and St Paul is mainly fourteenth-century. The unusual font appears to be made of two capitals — the bowl Norman and the base a little later. The village is attractive, with mainly seventeenth- and eighteenth-century stone houses either thatched or roofed with stone. The stocks and whipping post still stand on the village green, a reminder of the rough justice of earlier days. Just west of the village on the road to Teigh are the wharf buildings that were warehouses for the Melton to Oakham canal. After many difficulties in construction and funding the canal opened in 1802, only to close in 1847. It meandered eastwards from Melton towards Market Overton and thence southwards to Oakham; much of it is now without water.

MEDBOURNE

The Roman Gartree Road, which goes south-east from Leicester until it disappears just over the county border at Cottingham, passes by Medbourne, which was at the junction with a minor Roman road running east to west. There seems to have been a large market settlement here, which continued to be occupied in Anglo-Saxon times. It is still a comparatively large village and has some good stone building. The Old Hall is seventeenth-century, as is the exterior of the Manor, though inside is the original late thirteenth-century hall. A tributary of the river Welland flows through the village and is crossed near the church by a picturesque medieval bridge. The church, St Giles, is unusual for a village in that it has thirteenth-century transepts to the north and south, the southern having an eastern aisle. It may be that the church as a whole was intended to be much bigger, but only a south aisle was added, in the next century. The church was in an appalling state in the nineteenth century. The north transept had been badly altered in the seventeenth century to provide a schoolroom, which remained in use until 1869. This may account for the lack of anything of particular interest inside the church.

The medieval footbridge to Medbourne church.

MELTON MOWBRAY

Early closing Thursday; market days Tuesday and Saturday.

Melton, derived from 'Medeltone' meaning 'the dwelling in the middle of a district', is the principal town of the neighbourhood, with a market dating back to Saxon times. The manor was held by the Mowbrays from the end of the eleventh century for nearly four hundred years, hence the other element in the name. Its prosperity in the middle ages was founded on the wool trade and the wealthy merchants spent much money on the church, St Mary.

The base of the tower is Norman, but the main plan of the church dates from the years 1280 to 1330. It is unusually grand; it has not only a large nave with aisles, but a north and south transept, each with two aisles. From the exterior, however, what strike the eye are the fifteenth-century additions, for the nave and transepts were all given a magnificent clerestory and the upper stages of the tower were built. The church was restored in the 1850s and 1860s and the interior fittings are mainly Victorian. There are several monuments — a knight of about 1300, a late fourteenth-century lady and an incised slab to Sir John Pate, who

Melton Mowbray's noted pork-pie shop.

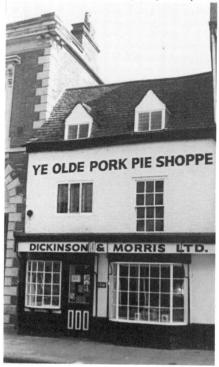

died in 1659, though it was probably made at the death of his wife, Elizabeth, in 1628.

Another medieval building is that in Burton Street known as Anne of Cleves' House. It dates from the fourteenth century, but has been extended in brick and most of the windows have been renewed in later centuries. Opposite is the Maison Dieu, an almshouse founded in 1640. Most of the other buildings in the town date from the eighteenth and nineteenth centuries. This was an era when Melton's fame rested not solely on its pork pies and Stilton cheese (see chapter 10) but on foxhunting. Melton Market Place is the neutral territory at the boundary of no less than three of the five hunts which make up the 'Shires'. The Belvoir hunts to the north, the Quorn to the west and the Cottesmore to the east. From the time of the Prince Regent, at whom snowballs were thrown for his miserliness in not tipping the bellringers of the town, to the present day the hunts have been patronised by royalty, and until the late 1930s members of the aristocracy flocked to Melton for the hunting season. They built hunting boxes on the outskirts of the town and spent the days hunting and the nights in drinking and adultery. The Marquis of Waterford was notorious for his 'practical jokes' and was responsible for 'painting the town red' in 1837. All prominent landmarks in the town, including the White Swan inn sign, were given a coat of red paint! Those days are past, and most of the hunting lodges are now occupied by commercial concerns.

MOUNTSORREL

Described in 1926 as 'a romantically named but singularly unattractive township', Mountsorrel straggles along the A6. There was once a castle that overlooked the main highway, but this was destroyed in 1217 and the hill on which it stood has been quarried for red granite. A market was granted in 1292 and, although markets are no longer held, the market cross, which was built in 1793, still stands, its domed roof supported by columns. Neither church is of any great interest, but a vicar built a splendid house for himself in 1782. It is a handsome red-brick building with a broad pediment surmounted by urns and decorated with ornamental drapery and garlands. Other humbler housing built of local materials may also be seen in the village.

NEWTOWN LINFORD

This was a new settlement from the village of Groby, founded some time in the thirteenth century, in a clearing of the then dense Charnwood Forest by a ford across the Lin stream. The small church is fourteenth-century, with a sixteenth-century north transept and nineteenth-century north aisle and

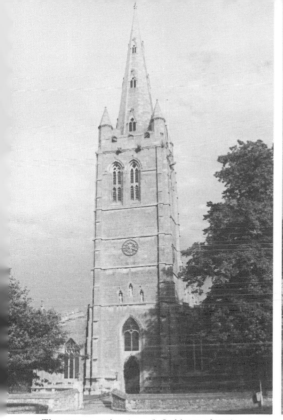

The tower and spire of Oakham church.

Mountsorrel: the market cross.

chancel. Over the chancel arch are the royal arms as they were in the eighteenth century, with the arms of the Grey family either side (see chapter 9). In the village are some attractive cruck cottages with thatched roofs. It is a popular place as one of the entrances to Bradgate Park (see chapter 2) is in the main street.

NORTH LUFFENHAM

The countryside around North Luffenham is very pleasant and the largely stone village blends in well. The church of St John Baptist was built in Norman times but rebuilt in the late thirteenth and early fourteenth centuries. The tower with its broach spire is of this period, as is the magnificent chancel, which still retains its original stained glass in one of the windows, and the double sedilia. The roof with its angels is a century or so later. There are an Elizabethan pulpit and several monuments, including one to Archdeacon Johnson, the founder of both Uppingham and Oakham schools, who died in 1625. The Hall, next to the church, dates back to the sixteenth century, with additions in each of the succeeding centuries. At the entrance is a fine seven-

teenth-century arch.

OADBY

Though it is still known to the older inhabitants as 'the village', Oadby is (in effect) the south-eastern suburb of Leicester, separated from it only by the racecourse. What was the heart of the old village has been rebuilt as a shopping centre to serve the ever increasing number of housing estates. The church, St Peter, was built at the beginning of the fourteenth century. The clerestory was added to heighten the nave about a hundred years later, raising it almost to the same height as the tower and thus lessening the impression made by the spire.

OAKHAM

Early closing Thursday; market days Wednesday and Saturday.

The county town of Rutland, although deprived of its administrative status in the local government reorganisation of 1974, is still a thriving centre for the surrounding countryside and well worth a few hours of any tourist's time. As well as the castle and the museum, described in chapters 5 and 6, All

61

The Butter Cross and stocks at Oakham.

Saints' church should be visited. The tall tower and spire were built in the fourteenth century and can be seen from almost anywhere in the town. The exterior of the large church is mainly fifteenth-century. Inside, however, is some thirteenth-century work — the south porch and north chapel — and the fine fourteenth-century carved capitals in the nave. That on the south side of the chancel arch shows Adam and Eve, the Annunciation and the Coronation of the Virgin; the western capital of the south side shows Reynard the Fox being pursued by Dame Malkin brandishing her distaff, while the monkey runs away (compare the scene at Tilton on the Hill, chapter 4).

Just north of the church is the original Grammar School, founded in 1584. The main buildings of the present public school are to the south of the church and are comparatively unobtrusive, unlike those at Uppingham. These are tucked behind the Market Place, which is the centre of the town and retains at one end the old Butter Cross. No market traders now shelter under its almost conical roof, but the stocks are still there. The earliest house in the town is in the High Street — Flore's House, dating back to the fourteenth century. Other interesting stone and brick houses may be seen in Church Street and Mill Street, and although there are no outstanding buildings Northgate Street with its stone and thatched cottages is particularly attractive.

QUORN

The full name of the village is Quorndon, that is the hill from which millstones (querns) were quarried, but it is more generally known by the shortened version. Its main claim to fame these days is that it has given its name to one of the finest hunts in Britain. Hugo Meynell, its founder, came to Quorn Hall in 1753 and, having kept his hounds for a few years at Great Bowden, soon brought them to Quorn. Here he established the hunting tradition of Leicestershire that despite opposition continues to this day. The kennels are now at Barrow upon Soar.

Earlier owners of Quorn Hall, the Farnham family, are commemorated in the church, St Bartholomew. There are four incised slabs, a wall monument and a very fine tomb chest with the effigies of John Farnham (died 1587) and his wife. The church is built of Mountsorrel granite and is mainly fourteenth-century with two reused Norman doorways.

ROTHLEY

Rothley is a village with a rich history. The earliest monument still standing is the ninth-century cross in the churchyard, unfortunately headless. Of the Norman church only the font remains, tub-shaped with a lozenge decoration. The present building dates from the thirteenth and fourteenth centuries, with an impressive tower and battlements on the nave and aisles. Inside are three incised slabs. That of Bartholomew Kyngston (died 1486) is unusual in that his will is engraved on it and takes up the top half, leaving little room for the rather foreshortened figures of the knight and his wife, Elyn. In the churchyard are a number of interesting tombstones of Swithland slate.

The village has several cruck cottages of the fifteenth and sixteenth centuries. Most of these are to be seen around Town Green. The most important house is Rothley Temple, now the Rothley Court Hotel. As its name suggests, it belonged to the Knights Templar, who were granted the manor in 1231 and, although the house has been altered considerably, the chapel is still much as it was when it was built sometime in the mid thirteenth century. The poet and historian Thomas Babington Macaulay was born here in 1800. He is perhaps little read these days, but his *Lays of Ancient Rome* and *History of England* were both bestsellers in Victorian times.

SHEPSHED
Market day Friday.

The village has always been quite large and expanded in the nineteenth century when framework knitting was the main occupation. Now that a junction of the M1 is so close it is even bigger, with more housing and industrial estates. The church is the oldest building, dating back to the thirteenth century, with the aisles added in the following century. Inside are some poppyhead bench ends of about 1500 and an interesting series of mainly eighteenth-century monuments to the Phillipps family, lords of the manor from 1561 to the present day. The reason that there are no later monuments to the family in the parish church is that Ambrose Phillipps de Lisle became a convert to Catholicism in 1824, at the age of fifteen. It was he who founded Mount St Bernard's Abbey (see chapter 4) and the original Roman Catholic church in Shepshed, both to designs by Pugin.

South of the church is the Bull Ring, which gets its name from the bull-baiting once so popular there, and in the surrounding streets may be seen several framework knitters' cottages and workshops. There are two mills on the outskirts of the village but neither is now in use. On the road to Hathern is a watermill attached to a farmhouse, which still retains its wheel though the mill race is now dry. On the A512 to Thringstone is a prominently sited windmill with two surviving sails, which has been converted into a private house.

SWITHLAND

The village consists of little more than one long main street but is one of several attractive villages in Charnwood Forest, having Victorian estate cottages and older thatched ones. The prime industry of Swithland in the seventeenth, eighteenth and early nineteenth centuries was the quarrying of slate, though this material was known and used for roofing even in Roman times. As well as roofing slates, which were always graded with the smallest at the top of a roof and the largest at the bottom, whole houses were built of it, and it was used for a variety of other purposes including cheese presses and especially gravestones. Many churches in the county have interesting collections of memorials, but some of the best are at Swithland itself. The most curious is a tomb-chest built half inside and half outside the churchyard. This arrangement was made so that Sir Joseph Danvers, who died in 1753, could have his favourite dog buried with him. Inside the church is a very fine wall monument of the mid eighteenth century in memory of five children of Sir John Danvers. The church, St Leonard, is mainly thirteenth-century with a south aisle built in 1727. The organ, made in 1765 by John Snetzler, has been well restored.

UPPINGHAM
Early closing Thursday; market day Friday.

Uppingham is Rutland's second town, slightly smaller than Oakham and with a rather different character. Like Oakham it has a school founded by Archdeacon Johnson, and the original school building is just south of the church. Its reputation and numbers increased greatly under the headmastership of the Reverend Edward Thring, appointed in 1853. He employed such distinguished architects as G. E. Street and Sir Thomas Jackson, whose buildings are in a more monumental style than those at Oakham. That and the fact that the school owns a lot of domestic property in High Street and London Road make it seem to dominate the town in a way that Oakham School does not.

The town is a very early settlement, dating from the sixth or seventh century, and was granted a market in 1281. The church of St Peter and St Paul is largely fourteenth-century, somewhat zealously restored and enlarged in 1860, but retains four demi-figures of about 1200 from an earlier building. These are very fine and show Christ blessing, two angels and a bearded saint. The Elizabethan pulpit is interesting, not only in itself but for the fact that it is probable that Jeremy Taylor, the noted Carolean divine and author of *Holy Living* and *Holy Dying*, preached from it during his time as Rector of Uppingham from 1637 to 1642. The church is on the south side of the Market Place and, although most of the buildings appear to be of the eighteenth or nineteenth centuries, many are actually seventeenth-century with later facades. A walk along High Street East and High Street West and their alleys is a delight for those interested

Left: *The main gateway to Uppingham School, with a statue of its founder, Archdeacon Johnson.*
Right: *The sign of the former Unicorn Inn at Uppingham.*

in domestic architecture from the eighteenth century onwards. Particularly noteworthy are the old Unicorn Inn, the Hall and Tudor House.

WIGSTON

Like Oadby, Wigston has been absorbed as a southern suburb of Leicester, with a modern shopping centre and more than its fair share of housing estates. It was known at one time as Wigston Two Steeples from its two churches. St Wistan's tower and spire date from the late thirteenth or early fourteenth century, but the rest of the church is entirely Victorian. The spire of All Saints church is about the same date as that at St Wistan's, but much more decorative, and the whole building is of this period. There are some odd little carvings on the capitals of the south aisle, and the nave roof of 1637 is worth seeing. The slender Georgian font is of alabaster. The few interesting houses are grouped around the church. In Bushloe End is a framework knitter's shop. The house is late seventeenth-century, cruck-built with eighteenth- and nineteenth-century alterations, and the two-storey workshop with long windows is behind it. The hand-frames are still in working order.

12
Tours for motorists

Route 1. Ashby de la Zouch, Moira, Appleby Magna, Appleby Parva, Twycross, Market Bosworth, Bosworth Field, Sutton Cheney, Cadeby, Ibstock, Donington le Heath, Ravenstone, Swannington, Ashby de la Zouch.
Route 2. Leicester, Houghton on the Hill, Ingarsby, Hungarton, Barsby, Gaddesby, Ashby Folville, Twyford, Burrough on the Hill, Owston, Launde, Tilton on the Hill, Billesdon, Gaulby, King's Norton, Little Stretton, Great Stretton, Leicester.
Route 3. Loughborough, Shepshed, Belton, Breedon on the Hill, Staunton Harold, Worthington, Osgathorpe, Grace Dieu, Mount St Bernard, Beacon Hill, Ulverscroft, Newtown Linford, Bradgate Park, Swithland,
Mountsorrel, Quorn, Loughborough.
Route 4. Market Harborough, Medbourne, Stoke Dry, Lyddington, Uppingham, Horninghold, Hallaton, Tur Langton, Church Langton, Foxton, Lubenham, Market Harborough.
Route 5. Melton Mowbray, Wymondham, Buckminster, Sproxton, Saltby, Croxton Kerrial, Knipton, Belvoir, Bottesford, Redmile, Plungar, Stathern, Eastwell, Ab Kettleby, Melton Mowbray.
Route 6. Oakham, Langham, Ashwell, Teigh, Market Overton, Cottesmore, Exton, Whitwell, Rutland Water, Empingham, Edith Weston, Normanton, North Luffenham, Morcott, Wing, Preston, Ridlington, Brooke, Oakham.

13
Tourist information centres

Ashby de la Zouch: Ashby de la Zouch Museum, 13-15 Lower Church Street, Ashby de la Zouch LE6 5ER. Telephone: 0530 415603.
Bosworth Battlefield: Bosworth Battlefield Visitor Centre, Sutton Cheney, Market Bosworth CV13 0AD. Telephone: 0455 292239.
Coalville: Public Library, High Street, Coalville LE6 2EA. Telephone: 0530 35951.
Hinckley: Public Library, Lancaster Road, Hinckley LE10 0AT. Telephone: 0455 30852 or 635106.
Leicester: Information Bureau, 25-27 St Martin's Walk, Leicester LE1 5DG. Telephone: 0533 511300.
Leicester: St Margaret's Bus Station, Leicester LE1 3TY. Telephone: 0533 532353.
Loughborough: John Storer House, Wards End, Loughborough LE11 3HA. Telephone: 0509 230131.
Market Harborough: Pen Lloyd Library, Adam and Eve Street, Market Harborough LE16 7LT. Telephone: 0858 62649 or 62699.
Melton Mowbray: Melton Carnegie Museum, Thorpe End, Melton Mowbray LE13 1RB. Telephone: 0664 69946.
Oakham: Public Library, Catmos Street, Oakham, Rutland LE15 6HW. Telephone: 0572 2918.

LEICESTERSHIRE AND RUTLAND

Bottesford +

Belvoir ▲
Castle

+ Eastwell

Buckminster ■

M■ MELTON
MOWBRAY

Gaddesby

I Wymondham

Teigh +

■ Market
Overton

O Rutland Railway
Museum

⊓ Burrough
Hill

■ Langham

+ Exton

Tolethorpe Hall
▲

OAKHAM
▲M■

Rutland
Water

+ Tickencote

I John o' Gaunt
Viaduct

Hungarton

⊓ Owston Abbey

Normanton Church
M Water Museum

ngarsby

+ Tilton on
the Hill

⊓ Sauvey
Castle

+ Brooke

Ketton ■

■ Billesdon

■ Launde

■ North
Luffenham

⊓ Wing

King's Norton

UPPINGHAM ■

Morcott I

Welland
Viaduct I

Horninghold
Hallaton ■   ⊓

+
Stoke Dry

+▲ Lyddington

Kibworth Harcourt

■ Church
Langton

■ Medbourne

I Foxton Locks

benham

M■ MARKET
HARBOROUGH

+

* Country park, etc (Ch.2)

⊓ Ancient monument (Ch.3)

+ Church (Ch.4)

▲ Historic building, garden (Ch.5)

M Museum (Ch.6)

I Industrial archaeology (Ch.7)

O Other place to visit (Ch.8)

■ Town, village (Ch.11)

67

Index

Page numbers in italic refer to illustrations.

Ambion 4
Anstey 34,*34*
Appleby Magna 48
Appleby Parva 48, *48*
Arnesby 34
Asfordby 5
Ashby de la Zouch 48, 49, 65
  Canal 36, 39
  Castle 4, 5, 20, *20*, 21, 22, 48
  Museum 26
Ashby Folville 4
Ashwell 40, 46
Atherstone Hunt 45
Aylestone 34, 49
Baggrave Hall 26, 51
Bakewell, Robert 41, *41*
Barrowden 42
Barrow upon Soar 3, 29, 45, 62
Barton in the Beans 30
Battlefield Line 8, 39
Beacon Hill 3, 7, *7*, 8
Beaumanor Park 7, 26
Belvoir Castle 4, 8, 20, *21*, 22, 45
Belvoir Hunt 45, 46, 60
Billesdon 11, 46, 49
Bosworth Battlefield 4, 8, 39, *39*, 57, 65
Bottesford 14, *14*
Bradgate Park *2*, 3, 7, 8, *8*, 42, 43, 61
Braunston 5
Breedon on the Hill 3, 4, *5*, 14, *15*, 27
  hillfort 3, 11
Brooke 14
Brooksby 42
Broombriggs Farm and Windmill Hill 8
Broughton Astley 42
Buckminster 49
Burnaby, Frederick 41
Burrough Hill 3, 8, 9, *10*, 11
Cadeby Light Railway 39
Cardigan, Earl of (James Brudenell) 6, 41
Castle Donington 4, 20, 49
Charles I, King 4, 20
Charnwood Forest 3, 7, 8, 10, 11, 60, 63
  Canal 5, 37, 38
Church Langton 8, 49
Claybrooke Mill 6, 35
Claybrooke Parva 15
Coalville 3, 5, 50, 65
Cook, Thomas 42, *42*
Cossington Hunt 45, 46, 60
Cranoe 41
Croxton Kerrial 3
Defoe, Daniel 5
Dishley 41
Donington Collection 26, 49
Donington le Heath Manor House 21, *22*
East Langton 49
East Midlands Aeropark 26, 49
Eastwell 15
Eaton 8
Edward IV, King 20
Empingham 4, *33*
Enderby 4, 49

Ermine Street 4
Exton 10, 15
Fenny Drayton 42
Ferneley, John 21, 28, 31, *32*
Fernie Hunt 45, 46, 59
Fosse Way 4, 8
Fox, George 42
Foxton Locks 3, 8, 35, *35*
Gaddesby 8, 15, *15*
Garendon Abbey 31
Gartree Road 4, 59
George III, King 41
Glooston 41
Goadby Marwood 4, 8
Grace Dieu Priory 11
Grand Union Canal 5, 34, 36
Grantham Canal *3*, 5
Great Bowden 47, 57, 62
Great Casterton 4, 29
Great Central Railway 34, 39
Great Glen 4
Great Stretton 4, 11
Greetham 10
Grey, Lady Jane 4, 7, 42, *61*
Groby 42, 60
Groby Pool 8
Gumley 4
Hallaton 8, 50, *50*
  Castle 4, 11, 50
Hamilton 12
Henry VII, King 4, 39
High Cross (*Venonis*) 4, 8
Hinckley 34, 51, 65
Horninghold 51
Hudson, Jeffery 43
Hungarton 51, *51*
Husbands Bosworth 3, 52, 57
Ibstock 52
Ingarsby 4, *11*, 12, 51
James I, King 20
John, King 13
John o'Gaunt Viaduct 35, *36*
Jubilee Way 8, 10
Kegworth 52
Ketton 3, 52, 55
Keyham 4
Kibworth Harcourt 3, 35, 57
King Lud's Entrenchments 10
Kings Norton 16, *17*
Kirby Muxloe Castle 3, 22, 22
Lambert, Daniel 29, 30, 43, *43*
Langham 52
Latimer, Hugh 4, 43
Launde 8, 52
Leicester 3, 4, 5, 11, 20, 30, 34, 35, 42, 43, 53, 59, 65
  Abbey 12, 45, 52
  All Saints 56
  Belgrave Hall *1*, 26
  Castle and Castle Gardens 4, 6, 54
  Cathedral, St Martin 26, 27, *54*, 55
  Clock Tower 53, *53*
  Donisthorpe and Company factory 36, *37*

Guildhall 26, *27*, 55
Holy Cross Priory 53
Holy Trinity 53
Jewry Wall 4, 12, *12*, 27, 54
Jewry Wall Museum 4, 27, *28*, 30, 54
John Doran Gas Museum 28, 35
Museum and Art Gallery 28, 54
Museum of Technology 29, *29*, 36
Museum of the Royal Leicestershire Regiment 30, 54
Newarke Houses Museum 30, 54
Raw Dykes 12
St Margaret 56
St Mary de Castro 54
St Nicholas 4, 12, 54, 55
Wygston's House Museum of Costume 27, *28*, 30, 55
Leicestershire Round 8
Leicester University Botanic Garden 23
Little Dalby 47
Lockington 16
Long Whatton 31
Loughborough 5, 9, 40, 42, 56, *56*, 65
  Bell Foundry Museum 30, *31*, 56
  Old Rectory Museum 31, 56
Lowesby 4
Lubenham 17
Lutterworth 5, 44, 57
Lyddington 13, 17
  Bede House 17, 23, *23*
Market Bosworth 8, 39, 42, 57
Market Bosworth Country Park 9
Market Harborough 35, 42, 57, *58*, 65
  Museum 31, 59
Market Overton 59
Marshall, Ben 29, 31, *43*
Mary, Queen of Scots 4, 20, 42
Medbourne 4, 6, 13, 51, 59, *59*
Melton Mowbray 5, 8, 11, 35, 41, 47, 60, *60*
  Carnegie Museum 28, 31, *32*, 65
Merrick, Joseph 43
Moira 5, 36, *37*, 48
Morcott *37*, 38
Mount St Bernard 17, 63
Mountsorrel 5, 8, 60, *61*
Newton Harcourt 57
Newton Linford 8, 60
Normanton Church Water Museum *cover*, 10, 32
North Luffenham 4, 61
Oadby 61, 64
Oakham 10, 43, 44, 45, 52, 61, *61*, *62*, 63, 65
  Canal 5, 59
  Castle 23, *25*, 62
  Rutland County Museum 32, *33*, 62

Rutland Farm Park 32
Oates, Titus 44
Osgathorpe 4
Outwoods 9
Owston Abbey 8, 13
Pickworth 4
Pork pies 31, 47, 60
Pytchley Hunt 45, 59
Quenby 47, 51
Quorn 45, 62
Quorn Hunt 41, 45, 46, 47, *47*, 49, 60, 62
Red Leicester cheese 47
Richard III, King 6, 20, 39, 57
Rothley 40, 62
Rupert, Prince 4, 12
Rutland Railway Museum 40, *40*
Rutland Water 6, 9, *9*, 10, 32
Sauvey Castle 4, 13
Scalford 4, 8
Seagrave 29
Seaton 38
Sewstern Lane 3, 10
Shackerstone 8, 39
Sharnford 4
Shepshed 63
Six Hills 3, 4
Soar, river 3, 34, 35, 36, 52
Somerby 41
Stanford Hall 24, *24*
  Motorcycle Museum 25, 33
Staunton Harold 17, *18*
Stilton cheese 31, 47, 60
Stoke Dry 18
Stoke Golding 18
Swannington 34, 35, 37
Swift, river 44
Swithland 63
Swithland slate 3, 10, 26, 34, 47, 52, 63
Swithland Woods 10
Teigh 18
Theddingworth 13
Thistleton 4, 10, 59
Thornton 8, 19
Thorpe Langton 49
Thrussington 31
Thurcaston 43
Thurmaston 4, 27
Tickencote 19
Tilton on the Hill 3, 19, 62
Tolethorpe Hall 25
Tropical Bird Garden 40
Tur Langton 49
Twycross 19
  Zoo 40
Ulverscroft Priory 13, 19, 45
Uppingham 61, 62, 63, *64*
Viking Way 8, 10
Waltham on the Wolds 5
Watling Street 4, 8
Welland Viaduct 38, *38*
West Langton 49
Whatborough 4
Whatton Gardens 25
Wigston 19, 64
Wing 13, *13*
Wistan, Saint 4, 19
Wistow 4, 19
Wreake, river 8
Wyclif, John 4, 44, *44*, 57
Wymondham 4, 38, 47